Promote Yourself!

DISCARD

Creating A Personal Promotion Plan For Your Career

DISCARD

By
Dave Marley

Silverpoint Press

SILVERPOINT

D1446058

Manufactured in the United States of America

**Publisher's Cataloging In Publication
(Provided by Quality Books, Inc.)**

Marley, Dave.
   Promote yourself! : creating a personal
promotion plan for your career / by Dave Marley.
-- 1st ed.
   p. cm.
   LCCN: 99-91797
   ISBN 0-945442-20-3

   1. Career development. 2. Success in business.
I. Title.

HF5381.M37 2000   650.14
                    QBI99-1940

Table of Contents

List of Exhibits

Chapter 1

Introduction

You wanted it. You worked for it. You think you deserved it. However, the promotion went to someone else.

Everyone has experienced this situation in their career and it may make us not only begin to doubt the fairness of our company's promotion practices – but also our own abilities.

However, the loss of a promotion is not necessarily an indication that the company has no confidence in you. It might just be that you were more needed in your current position; it may be that the promoted employee has superior skills, not visible to you; it may even be that your management correctly understands that you are not ready for a promotion.

> **While all of these reasons may be possible, in all too many cases people are not promoted because the persons making the decisions simply don't know enough about them and their talents.**

It would be nice if corporate decision-making were always based on sound logic and complete information. However, no one who has worked corporate America believes this is always the case. There is a hard reality about advancement in corporate America -- and in advancement in our society in general.

> **All too often, the most important decisions about your career are made at times you haven't anticipated, in places where you are not present, by people who don't know you well.**

This is not a result of some evil plot. It is not that companies wish to promote the wrong people. It is just a simple fact that all corporate decision-making is made under pressure, with imperfect information.

In addition, promotion decisions are usually *group* decisions. Your abilities may be well known by one or two members of the executive group, but if your talents and experience are invisible to their fellow executives, you may lose out to a less capable, but better-known, co-worker.

Significant corporate changes – and the promotions that commonly follow them, usually involve more than one position, so the entire executive team may be involved in making promotion decisions. Most of the executive team is likely to be unfamiliar with your day-to-day activities.

> **They will judge you by your personal and professional reputation; by your demeanor; by written and verbal presentations you have made; by what they have heard your co-workers say about you.**

This book alone cannot make you into a superior employee or promise you unlimited success. Nor can it assure that you have the *will* to succeed. These are personal qualities that you either must have or must develop.

> **What this book is designed to deliver is the condition that if you fail, it will not be a failure of <u>notice</u>. This book will give you the tools you need to <u>promote your career</u>, by <u>promoting yourself</u>.**

The word *promotion* in a personal context is used just as it would be with any other product or service you are trying to sell. The need is similar. The tools are similar. The results can be predicted.

> **Your objective is to ensure that the company and all its managers understand the contributions you are making, and the additional contributions you might make if given the opportunity of career advancement**

There is nothing unethical or devious about applying the same talents you use to market your company's products and services to marketing your career. The reality is that *your success* is necessary for *your company's success*. Companies do not grow with incompetent or passive employees. Companies want to invest in their best performers.

> **Salaries and promotions and perks are corporate resources with the same requirements and limitations as any other company assets. They must be properly allocated in order for the company to grow.**

Personal promotion for advancement is not only valid for corporate employees, but also for entrepreneurs, independent workers, salespeople, and the managers of non-profit organizations.

Budding politicians? Of course. Politicians may be the consummate practitioners of personal promotion. They know better than anyone that their *personal advancement* is only available through *personal promotion*.

For non-corporate workers, the critical judgments of others may not be as direct as those within a corporation, but just as critical for advancement. Customers, vendors, competitors, the public-at-large, all play a role in determining whether someone is a success.

In many ways, personal promotion for entrepreneurs and independent workers is even more important. The people upon whom you are dependent for success are even less likely than a corporate supervisor to know you well. In the world of the professional and the entrepreneur, there is no corporate mandate that others objectively evaluate your performance and manage your progress. Initiating these things is your sole responsibility.

Fortunately, the tools of personal promotion are the same whether or not you are deep in the bowels of a large corporation or working in the field every day, supported only on your laptop, cell phone and pager.

The most important tools you bring to your personal promotion effort are the talents you use everyday in building business. Communications, awareness, knowledge of people and events are all necessary for any type of promotional activity -- including a personal promotion campaign.

Build Your Professional Equity

We all understand the concept of building equity in a home or a business. The equity is that portion of the asset that you own – independent of the claims of others.

Even as a corporate employee you need to work to build equity in yourself – and your career. Your equity in your career is the value you own, independent of your current position. Your desk, your chairs, your computer and your title – your employer owns all these things.

When you focus on building professional equity, you focus on those things that build your unique value to your employer – and to your next employer. You can take these assets with you to any job you may accept. You can define your professional equity as:

- ☑ Your education
- ☑ Your knowledge
- ☑ Your interpersonal skills
- ☑ Your professional relationships
- ☑ Your professional skills
- ☑ Your professional reputation
- ☑ Your professional visibility
- ☑ Your breadth of experience
- ☑ Your ethical standards

You own these valuable assets. Build and enhance their value with an effective personal promotion plan.

Planning

Everyone accepts the necessity for planning in corporate activities. Budgets, marketing plans, campaigns, these are all essential tools for success in business.

But how many people have a plan for their advancement? Not a dream, not a wish, not a few vague aspirations as to what their future will be -- a plan with clear objectives, strategies, tactics, committed resources, and timelines.

> **Don't prepare one more business plan until you have prepared a personal promotion plan for yourself.**

The first essential for any plan is that it must be in writing. It is only by writing the plan that you force yourself to commit to clear courses of action. A written plan makes it easier for you to spot discrepancies and conflicts between your objectives and strategies. *A written plan represents commitment.*

Everyone is familiar with the basics of any plan: objectives, strategies, tactics, and a budget (resources). When you review the recommendations you find in this book, consider each of them as to how they may be useful in preparing your personal plan.

How you may adapt them to meet your personal objectives. How you may build upon them to fit the resources you have available.

The Right Tools

There is one major difference between your personal promotion and a corporate business plan: you don't have the same level of resources at your disposal. However, this does not mean that you don't have *significant resources* at your disposal. Today's technology – the computer, laser printers, the Internet, has put communication tools in the hand of the individual that corporate managers only dreamed about twenty years ago.

A cynic once remarked, "the power of the press belongs to those who own one." Today almost everyone owns a digital "press." It may be used for publishing books, monographs, direct mail campaigns, audio and videocassettes, or web pages. It can even be employed to build that most powerful corporate weapon -- a well written E-mail or memo. The tools of personal promotion are powerful and can be pervasive. They are available to anyone that wants to know how to use them.

Awareness Is The Foundation

An ambitious corporate employee has four primary targets for personal promotional efforts: the company, customer\prospects, the industry and the community. An entrepreneur has three primary targets: customers\ prospects, the industry and the community.

> **Personal promotion must have more than one focus. It is not enough to simply promote yourself inside the company where you are currently employed. All too often today, companies fail, they are merged, they redirect themselves (and their employees) to different markets and industries.**

A successful individual prepares a personal promotion plans that accommodates all these possibilities.

Awareness in the company is obvious. It ensures that your co-workers and your supervisors understand your capabilities and the contribution you are making.

Awareness in the industry promotes your talents among customers, vendors, and industry leaders. This can assist you in making sales, in being seen as an industry leader, and most important, being considered for new job opportunities that may become available outside your company.

Awareness in the community exposes your talents in new areas and to people not a part of a parochial industry. Perhaps you are destined to succeed in an area totally different from your current industry. In addition, community activities give you a break from the narrow focus of most businesses, as well as allow you to improve the community environment for yourself and your family.

Mom Taught You To Always Be Modest -- Mom Was Wrong

For most people, promoting themselves, their accomplishments and their abilities may be somewhat uncomfortable. Much of the culture in our country is based on personal modesty and *doing good* whether or not you are *seen to be doing good.*

However, it is necessary to separate those qualities that may be *admirable in your personal life* from those that are *necessary in your public life.* Certainly, no one wants to be around people who incessantly brag about themselves. That is not the objective for the personal promotion campaign described in this book.

Personal promotion is an effort to assure that your talents, efforts and skills are recognized and properly applied for the success of yourself, your company and your community.

Always remember that if you do not match *personal performance* with *personal promotion,* your success in obtaining greater visibility may only hasten recognition that you are not qualified for advancement.

Chapter 2

Benefits from Personal Promotion

There is room at the top for only a few.

Twenty years ago Al Ries popularized the concept of "positioning." This is a powerful and useful tool for analyzing not only products, but also promotable employees. It's based on the premise that people -- consumers or supervisors, are always working to classify information into a structured order. Their ability to keep track of information is finite. Consequently, they have room in specific categories for only a few candidates.

Ask a consumer for the "best" coffee, bread, jam, stereos, etc., and they will likely only be able to name two or three choices. Ask a supervisor the candidates that are most likely to be selected for promotion and the supervisor is likely to name two or three possibilities – not the entire junior management class.

Corporate promotions always require selecting the few from among the many.

It is not that managers do not think about who is promotable among their employees. This is generally a high priority for effective managers. Its just that few managers consider all their employees as candidates for promotion. They generally shift a small group of people in and out of what they identify as the "promotable" group.

Some are shifted in and out as they demonstrate growth or decline in their abilities. Some are considered or not considered because the needs of the company change and therefore the type of employee needed changes.

Some employees are not considered simply because the managers do not know enough about those employees. Managers must have confidence in the character and the ability of the people they promote. But before there can be confidence built, there must be awareness and this is a primary objective of your personal promotion activities.

Many companies appear to settle on a certain type of "promotable" employee. This may be based on a particular college degree or type of training, mastering of a particular set of skills such as computer tools or quantitative analysis, or even a particular personality type.

It is important to identify this trait in a company so that you can select which of your personal attributes are best for your personal promotion efforts.

Corporate rules or practices for promotion are not ironclad. Special events or crises can cause companies to break out of their old routines in order to seek promotable employees.

Corporate crises are among the best opportunities for personal advancement. The need may be urgent. Old habits and restrictions may be relaxed. Managers may be more willing to take chances on employees that are unproven or that do not clearly meet the old requirements.

Employees should always be sensitive to times of corporate crises and view these not only as an opportunity to assist the company, but also as an opportunity to demonstrate personal skills and talents that may not previously have been apparent.

Promotion Opportunities Vary Between Groups Within A Company.

It is a mistake to think that promotion decisions throughout a company are monolithic and made by some common standard. They are very much influenced by the personality of the person in charge of a particular activity, by the history of that corporate activity, and by the value that is placed on that activity by corporate management.

In many cases, the best thing you can do to promote your career is to move from a corporate backwater to an area of more immediate management interest.

Of course, this may involve additional risk to your career. The potential for reward may be higher but the penalties for failure may be more severe.

What Type Of Employee Are You?

Whether you are growing from a child to an adult or a college student to a successful employee, you learn that the world tends to classify everything into "types." There is much talk within companies about types of employees and types of individuals.

Consciously or unconsciously, ambitious employees identify certain types of individuals as more or less successful within the company. They may try to modify their behavior and activities to fit this success model. In addition, it's fun to try to classify co-workers into "types" of employee. Exhibit 2A describes some of these "types."

> **The reality is that we are all a combination of several types of personalities. And whatever type(s) we were when we began our career, may change as we mature and gain new experience.**

What type you are, is not as important as what qualities you offer to your company and the broader communities in which you participate. What companies want from any type of employee are positive contributions:

- ☑ People who contribute to the limits of their abilities
- ☑ People who can solve problems
- ☑ People who can marshal and manage resources in the most economical way
- ☑ People who can lead the company to success.

Exhibit 2A: Descriptions Of Typical Employee Types

The drudge
- ☑ Every supervisor's dream as an employee
- ☑ Rarely considered for senior position
- ☑ Believes that all problems yield to maximum effort
- ☑ Would rather work than think
- ☑ Believes that success is always a result of hard work

The Scholar
- ☑ Every teacher's favorite
- ☑ Focuses on intellectual purity
- ☑ Would rather be right than successful
- ☑ Makes an excellent staff employee
- ☑ Has great confidence in the value of additional information
- ☑ Has difficulty focusing on the most critical elements in a decisions
- ☑ Believes there is always one best answer to every problem

The Kamikaze
- ☑ Every Drill Sergeant's favorite
- ☑ Sees every problem as a crisis
- ☑ Has little regard for planning and intellectual problem-solving
- ☑ An adrenaline freak
- ☑ Believes quick and aggressive action is key to success

The Joker\Comedian
- ☑ The co-worker's favorite
- ☑ Would rather have a laugh than a promotion
- ☑ Sometimes forgets when humor is inappropriate
- ☑ Believes no 'straight line" should go unanswered

The Clothes Horse\GQ Guy-Glamour Gal
- ☑ The mall retailer's favorite
- ☑ Believes that looking like a manager is as good as being a manager
- ☑ Will do anything for the company, so long as they don't get mussed
- ☑ Believes thinking to be an unnecessary distraction – and you might get wrinkles

The Priest\Confidant
- ☑ The favorite of the problem-burdened
- ☑ Everyone's shoulder to cry on
- ☑ Good for free donuts in the morning
- ☑ Believes co-workers' problems are much more interesting than business problems

The Flower Child
- ☑ Careful not to get stained by the crassness of capitalism
- ☑ Glad to work at their job -- so long as it doesn't last too long, is fair to all, and the break room has a refrigerator for their yogurt
- ☑ Would be stunned if promoted
- ☑ Believes that they are just passing through

The Efficiency Expert
- ☑ The consultant's favorite
- ☑ Has an analytical tool for every problem
- ☑ Sees people as just variables in his equations
- ☑ Believes people to be just an unnecessary obstacle to the perfect solution

Visible Success Builds Management Confidence In Your Capabilities

While employees generally consider promotion opportunities only as something that affects them, it can also have a very serious effect on the managers that offer the promotion. There are risks involved for the company. You may fail. *Your failure* may be seen as *your managers' failure.*

> **Promoting you requires a "leap of faith" by your managers.**

When they decide to promote you they are allocating some of the company's scarce resources. They are closing off opportunities to promote and therefore utilize the talents of other promotable employees. They are indicating that the qualities and skills you have meet the standards they have for promotable employees.

> **Most managers are as insecure as their subordinates. They want to do well in their career. They also want to be promoted.**

More importantly for your plan of personal promotion, they can be influenced by the opinion of other supervisors and even of your co-workers. In the case of other managers, your manager wants a promotion decision to be seen as the right thing to do, and as a good use of corporate resources.

Do Your Co-workers See You As A Leader

Your co-workers may be competitors for your next promotion, but they also can be important allies. Everyone knows individuals that are identified as "natural leaders," even though it's not clear that there is anything such as a "natural leader."

However, there are individuals who seem to be easily accepted by their co-workers as persons they are willing to follow. They not only demonstrate certain professional capabilities, but an interest in their co-workers and a willingness to reciprocate in matters of mutual assistance.

If it appears your promotion will be accepted by your co-workers, your managers may be more comfortable promoting you to supervise them.

Do Your Company's Clients See You As A Leader?

Every company has clients upon whom it is dependent for success. It doesn't matter whether these clients are consumers, other companies, or government entities. Companies must satisfy these clients in order to succeed.

Naturally if a company's executives see evidence that a company's clients have a particular appreciation for one of the company's employees, they also will place a higher value on that employee. This is one of the most powerful advantages of personal promotion efforts that are targeted outside the company.

Building Credibility For Yourself Builds Credibility For Your Company

Visible success within the industry also can identify you as a leader. Perhaps the most obvious reason for building visibility within an industry is so that you will be considered for promotion opportunities -- not only within your current company, but also by other companies as well.

In today's world of downsizing, layoffs, cutbacks and reorganizations, it is a foolish employee that focuses all personal promotion activities on a single company.

> **Employees have come to see that managing their career within a profession or industry is just as important as managing their career within a company.**

In addition, it is even more difficult for persons outside your company to see that you are "promotable." This makes the "mass media" tools of personal promotion all the more important.

You must use these tools to reach outside your immediate circles to assure that your talents are visible to more than your immediate supervisor and your company's senior management. They must be visible to the community at large.

A Successful Individual Suggests An Individual That Creates Successful Corporations

We all know people that seem to be able to do everything well. Things look easy for them. Rewards seem to come easily. However, this is probably not true. These people are likely to work as hard as any others to achieve success. It is just that their efforts may be less visible to you.

The reality is that people that have demonstrated success in <u>any area</u> of their life are often assumed to be capable of success in <u>all areas</u> of their life.

To corporate managers, success that is visible to people outside the company enhances one's value as a candidate for opportunities inside the company.

In addition, individual success outside the company reflects credit on the company. If you help the company improve its visibility within the community or within the industry, you are helping the company succeed. The experience you gain in the community and outside the company may be applied to resolve the same types of problems and situations that you find inside the company.

Companies Promote People Based on the Expectation of Future Successes.

Rarely is a promotion simply a bigger version of your current job. There are new responsibilities, new subordinates, and new resources at your disposal. Few jobs will prepare you one hundred percent for the next promotion. This is why promotions require the "leap of faith" from your managers discussed earlier. But your success within the community and the industry builds the confidence of your managers that you have the talents to meet their future needs.

Promotions Are Based On The Needs Of The Company, Not The Employee

A frequent misconception by young employees is that promotions are a rational and orderly process within a company. Employment brochures and human resources departments often perpetuate this illusion. Training programs hold out the promise that if employees do good work, follow the prescribed training programs and work hard, advancement is almost automatic.

> **The hard reality is that companies promote people when the company has a job that needs doing, not necessarily when the employee is ready for a promotion.**

Any opportunity or job that is one hundred percent predictable is a job not worth having. No one can promise you that if you take certain actions and behave in a certain way promotion will be automatic. You must manage your own career and your own preparation for future opportunities.

The cycle of corporate need for promotable individuals is likely to be erratic and unpredictable.

When your talents and experiences quality you for promotion there may be no promotion opportunities. Conversely, when the next promotion opportunity arises you may not be fully ready for promotion. Either of these situations may deny you a promotion.

However, your objective should be to ensure when the opportunity arises you are as prepared as you possibly can be and most important, that the people making the promotion decision are fully aware of your availability and your capabilities.

Chapter 3

Organizing Your Promotional Effort

Earlier in these pages we discussed the need for creation of a plan for personal promotion. Like any good plan, this requires consideration of both the task before you and the talents you bring to this work.

The first lesson to be learned is simple. Persuasive promotion is not a substitute for persuasive performance.

Its long been known in advertising circles that effective ads can cause poor products to fail even more rapidly. Promotion and communication increase visibility and increased "trial." The quicker people try a product and reject it, the quicker it will fail. In a like manner, high visibility of mediocre performance may only hasten an employee's decline.

What your personal promotion plan is going to assure is that you achieve the success you are capable of earning and not a success based on some false perception your managers may have of you.

The reality today is that everyone does *good work*. What you want to do is *exemplary work*.

This doesn't mean that some super human employee is the most likely candidate for promotion. It's not that simple. Good work is judged not only by talent you have, but also by judgment, proper application, attitude, and most important, company need.

Success Is Not Just Delivering The Most Widgets

The simplified measure of success is the person who produces the greatest quantity of some objectively measured item. Rarely is this the only criteria.

☑ **Do you have your manager's confidence?** – Remember the risk factor in a manager's promotions. Prudent managers don't want a loose cannon on their team. Managers must have your confidence that when they are not there to closely supervise, you can be trusted to do the right thing.

☑ **Can you lead a team?** – Even expert surgeons need a surgical team. There are few important jobs that can be done by a single individual. If you cannot muster and manage the talents of fellow employees you are unlikely to be able to accomplish important tasks.

☑ **Can you write a plan?** – Your managers, your co-workers, your team, all need clear guidelines as to what is the task to be accomplished and how it will be undertaken. A plan is essential. It must be focused on the objectives at hand, consistent with the resources available to you, and understandable to the people who must execute it.

☑ **Do you have your manager's perspective?** – Your managers will judge your success by how closely you meet *their* standards, not *your* standards. You may know a better way, but it is your job to convince your managers of that fact before you undertake your new way. Managers want predictable results and that means results consistent with their objectives and standards.

☑ **Have you acquired the necessary skills for the job you want, rather than the job you have?** –The tools that have made you a success in your present job – in your eyes the reason for your success, may not be what you need for the next job. Remember that promotions are based on what you can deliver in the future and not what you are delivering today. Always take advantage of company training opportunities whether it if for simple desktop computer skills or executive management programs.

☑ **Is your success visible to more than your manager?** – If you are doing a good job in your present position your promotion may not be in the best interest of your manager. Upon your promotion, a valuable subordinate will be lost. A replacement must be found. Production will suffer. You may become a competitor at your manager's level. It's amazing that anyone gets promoted at all!

The reality is that most promotions are pushed upon managers by higher managers. They are the ones who have the need to find promotable employees to meet corporate needs. Your immediate manager may be perfectly happy for these promotions to go to some one in another department. This is an important reason why effective personal promotion an essential component in anyone's career plans.

Defining Events For Success.

We have already discussed that the cycle of corporate needs may not match the cycle of your personal needs. However, it may be possible to *bend* the cycle of corporate needs to your advantage. There are situations that create opportunities for success.

Obviously consistently superior performance is the best tool you can have in your tool case. However, it is important to recognize that something less than superior performance may be accepted under the right circumstances.

☑ **Company crises** –There is nothing more likely to cause senior management to cast about for new solutions (i.e. new managers) than a corporate crisis. Sales are down. A key client is unhappy. A natural disaster has hit corporate facilities. A competitor has introduced a significant new product. A key manager has defected to a competitor.

Any such crisis can create an opportunity for you. That is, if you have properly executed your personal promotion plan so that management is *aware* of your capabilities.

☑ **Special Projects** – Special projects are just a more leisurely form of company crises. They generally are designed to solve a *nagging* company problem rather than an *unexpected* one. They often offer high visibility for extra work. They may provide the opportunity for you to display talents outside the realm of your day-to-day activities.

The first requirement is to be selected for the project team. Ideally you would want to be the project leader. If this opportunity is not offered you, volunteer to a member of the project team.

☑ **Introduction of new products and services** – Most people's day-to-day activities are occupied by just delivering existing products. New products create new strains and requirements to be met. However, they also offer chances for visibility.

☑ **Satisfying significant clients** –This generally means satisfying *unhappy*, significant clients. Few opportunities are available if there is a smooth relationship with large clients. Someone has already taken advantage of these opportunities and will be firmly entrenched.

It is the ugly situations where opportunities arise. These can be significant even if you fail to resolve the current conflicts. You may demonstrate to your management, talents that can be effectively employed with other clients and in other opportunities.

Identifying Gatekeepers To Success.

Just as you want to plan to organize your activities you need a plan to identify and focus on the gatekeepers to personal success. Identifying these gatekeepers, selecting tools to approach them, and setting up a mutually beneficial relationship is a key part of the planning and organization of your personal promotion plan. We will review these gatekeepers in more detail in Chapter 4.

Are You A Brand?

Recently, it has become popular to advise ambitious people to market themselves as "brands." That's right, just like COCA-COLA® and NABISCO®, or with more glamour, BMW® and NIKE®.

The branding argument is similar to some of the advice in this book: influence what people think of you, make yourself visible, position yourself for advancement.

However, these "personal branders" are a little more direct. They want your audiences to have a clear opinion of what they can expect from you, by virtue of the "brand" you have assumed for yourself. They believe that people will more quickly hire an applicant for a position that is projecting a brand that clearly reflects what they desire for an open position.

The question that should be of concern about personal "brands" is whether they may be useful in the short term, but too limiting for the long term.

Your expectations for a cookie or soft drink are very much the same today as when you first experienced them as a child. The brand assures you of their quality -- *and their consistency.* New jobs, new challenges, new bosses, are likely to require different qualities from you over time.

Most people will have several different careers during their working life. It's not likely a single "brand" will serve equally well for all the positions you will be asked to fill.

Why not just change "your brand" as circumstances dictate? Is this desirable or even possible? Have we forgotten the New Coke?

Will people trust the seriousness of a person that takes on a personal brand or image as readily as a new fashion in clothes?

In another part of this book, the argument will be made that a personal promotion plan should be *visible only to you.* Your prospective employers and supervisors will not be comfortable with an employee that appears to have more interest in personal posturing than corporate problem solving.

A concept (described in Chapter One) more comfortable for me than personal branding, is the idea of building your 'Professional Equity." The steps and efforts necessary to build this "equity" will be mutually advantageous to you and your company.

The benefits will be similar to personal branding. The difference is that the resources you assemble as a part of your Professional Equity, will serve you well in any situation. New challenges won't require a new brand.

Would You Promote Your Manager?

A final element in organizing your personal promotion effort involves a critical analysis of your current manager. It's possible that you are working for a manager who cannot recognize good work. It may be that you can see that the standards under which your manager operates are clearly in conflict with the overall standards of the company. Some managers are held in such low regard within a company that their subordinates are also assumed to be incompetent.

> **Finally, some managers just don't want their subordinates to succeed. It is the zero-sum mentality. They believe there is a fixed amount of success and if you do well, then they must do less well.**

This type of situation is corrosive to personal success. If you find yourself with this type of manager the first step in any personal promotion plan has got to be to find a new home – either within the company or at another company. Don't waste your time in trying to correct impossible situations.

How do you know the difference between a bad boss and a boss that is just demanding? The best advice is to just trust your instincts. Are you enduring circumstances in your job that you would not tolerate in other areas of your life? If so, you probably shouldn't tolerate them in you supervisor. Exhibit 3A offers some clues that you might use to judge your situation – and your boss.

You should also recognize that no boss is perfect or always able to be wise, patient, and caring. Everybody has bad days and makes mistakes.

However, you should judge your boss just like any other obstacle to your personal promotion plan. If it can't be fixed, go around it!

Exhibit 3A: How To Recognize A Bad Boss

☑ Is your boss verbally abusive to you or any other subordinate, beyond any semblance of efforts to correct the poor performance of subordinates?

☑ Does your boss give proper credit to subordinates for their work, or always take personal credit for the work done in your department?

☑ Does your boss display any interest in your personal life, or give other indications that s\he recognizes that you have a life outside of work?

☑ Does s\he introduce you to visitors to your department or ignore you as s\he would any other piece of department equipment?

☑ Does s\he directly acknowledge to you the value of your work to the department and company?

☑ Does s\he simply criticize your work or use corrections to explain how you can do your job better?

☑ And my favorite tip-off for recognizing a bad boss: Does s\he treat service people – wait persons, cleaning personnel, clerks, admin assistants, and stewardesses, with respect and courtesy or abuse and indifference?

Chapter 4

Internal Targets
Of Promotional Focus

It's obvious that if you want a promotion that is only available through your company's management, this group must be the primary focus of your promotional efforts. The problem is that most senior managers spend much of their days being pitched some proposal or another, so that they have developed a very keen B.S. filter to separate the messages they receive.

> **The fact that you want notice from senior management does not mean that they will offer it. You must give clear evidence to them that you deserve <u>their notice</u> by providing solutions <u>to their problems</u>.**

Attracting Your Management's Notice

The first step is for you to identify what are the most likely subjects to be of interest to management. Is it declining profits, declining sales, personnel problems, incompetent subordinates, problems with the board of directors, some ambition in the community that is being unmet? Not all of these interests will be obvious, but some will be.

Defining the personal interests of the executives you wish to notice you will suggest ways to approach them. It is through these activities that you can demonstrate your value to management. Consider these possibilities to approach your management:

☑ **Speech outlines\Speeches** –Most executives are regularly faced with the need to present speeches to clients, Boards of Directors and industry meetings. Few executives like to write these speeches.

If you have the talent to write speeches you will find your talents always in demand. If you do not have the talents to write an effective speech you may be able to outline and research the information needed for the executive to write the speech.

Subjects of interest are most likely to be new techniques or services that the company has to offer, hot topics in the industry, and speeches that give an overall presentation of the company's capabilities.

☑ **White papers** –Every industry has periodic needs for additional information on specific subjects. Generally, these are new techniques or trends or ideas in which everyone has an interest, but for which no one feels they have sufficient information.

Providing this information to a key executive can be done by a "white paper" written by you. Creative writing ability is not required, simply the ability to gather information and present it clearly to a reader.

☑ **FAQs/Description sheets** – All companies periodically create new products and services. Often there is a delay in producing sufficient descriptive information for the use of company employees. As an employee, you are likely to have to learn this information for your own use. Why not capture it on paper as "Frequently Asked Questions," and make it available to management and fellow employees. You will demonstrate initiative as well as comprehensive knowledge about some new event.

☑ **Special presentations** –A more graphic form of the FAQ is a visual presentation on the new product or service or technique. While succinctly and effectively writing presentations is a little more difficult than writing FAQs, it is still an easy enough talent to develop. More importantly, you may even have the opportunity to personally deliver a presentation where you might only be asked to mail or E-mail an FAQ.

☑ **Be an authority** –As you work to provide the materials described above, you very well may become identified as the "authority" on a new problem or practice. This not only can increase the value of your contributions in the eyes of management, but may also help you in adding value to your relationship with co-workers.

☑ **Industry calendars** – It's a simple task to prepare a calendar of significant industry and corporate events and make this available to your management and co-workers. The wide availability of desktop computing tools and their digital calendars provides the perfect avenue to distribute these tools.

☑ **Glossaries** – Where would any industry be without its buzzwords and acronyms? Your publishing such a glossary not only will be a valuable tool for new employees but may give you the opportunity to seek out people in the company you might not ordinarily encounter to order to build and improve your glossary. Additions to the glossary give you opportunities to distribute revised glossaries, calling additional attention to your activities.

☑ **Be a news photographer** –You can describe events on paper in FAQs and presentations and white papers. But, you can save "a thousand words" by sending a picture.

The digital imaging tools commonly available today provide presentation tools that were only dreamed of a few years ago.

Capture these images with a digital camera or utilize photofinishing services available in any photo shop or drug store to convert ordinary 35mm snapshots into digital images.

Once you have digital images you may move them freely by E-mail within the company and within the industry.

☑ **Convention correspondent** –If you are lucky enough to be sent to an industry convention, don't just spend the time satisfying your own need for new information. Prepare a summary of what you see, what you feel, what you experience -- about the industry and the event.

Don't wait until you return home. Skip the heavy dinners and bars and in-room movies. Prepare a report to your managers, your clients and your co-workers.

Use your digital imaging tools to add impact to your report. Interpret what you see. Draw conclusions that demonstrate your judgment to your management. Make suggestions. Pose provocative questions that may invite discussions with senior management upon your return.

Key Co-workers

No one succeeds without some help from co-workers. You need their support, their cooperation, and their information. Consider who are your key co-workers, how they can help your personal promotion plan – and how you can help them.

☑ **Your boss** – Most people would mistakenly identify their boss as their most important focus for personal promotion. This is rarely the case. It is actually your boss's boss that should be your primary concern. Remember your boss has a great deal to lose by your being promoted.

Nevertheless, your boss at least must not be hostile to your efforts to advance. You need to ensure that your efforts are positioned in ways that your boss is able to identify some personal advantage to her.

☑ **Your boss's boss** – The best avenue to get around any limitations placed upon you by your boss, is to impress your boss's boss. In addition, your boss's boss is one step higher up the corporate ladder. S\he is one step closer to the other corporate executives that you wish to make aware of your activities.

☑ **Your company's key executives** – This is the group that will likely be involved in any corporate reorganization. This is the group that you must impress that is least aware of your day-to-day successes. The best tool you have to correct this absence of awareness is your personal promotion plan.

☑ **Executive Administrative Assistants** – Being nice to some executive's secretary is hardly an original idea. In fact, executive secretaries have a B.S. filter almost equal to that of their supervisors. They know their primary loyalty is to their boss and they will not allow any relationship with you to endanger that.

However, they are not immune to offers of assistance. Many executives have long since forgotten how to actually make something happen. They are accustomed to simply issuing commands to other executives or to their executive assistant in order to take some action.

When an executive secretary calls for assistance, be responsive, be polite, and be helpful. Oftentimes it will just be a request to identify the right person or the right tool. Do whatever you can. It is likely that the favor will be reciprocated at some point in the future.

☑ **Financial Officers** –Being in charge of protecting a company's financial assets is not much fun. Most of your day is filled with encounters with co-workers trying to scatter the company's wealth among their pet projects. All too often you become the "Grinch" that steals someone's ambitious plan.

However, satisfying the requirements of your financial officer is necessary for the success of any project or plan of interest to you. Not only must the resources be available, but also the financial officer must be persuaded that this is the proper use of the company's funds.

It's possible to convince a senior executive to overrule a financial officer as to the potential value of a proposal, but it's not a task you want to undertake if it can be avoided.

☑ **Receptionists** –Receptionists get my vote for the most underpaid and under appreciated employees in a company. The routine is mind numbing, the interruptions are constant, and respect is often lacking. Being nice to a receptionist often means no more than not causing them unnecessary aggravation.

Let them know where you can be found. Don't expect them to screen your calls if you don't have an administrative assistant. Don't embarrass them by keeping visitors waiting at their desks for extended periods of time. A good relationship with your receptionist can mean the difference between an important caller hearing "Mr. Jones doesn't answer and I don't' know where he is " and "Mr. Jones is in a meeting now, may I please take a message?"

Building Your Personal Network

Business associates, whether inside or outside the company, are the building blocks of your personal, professional network. These are individuals outside your direct chain of command that you depend upon for support, information, assistance, advice and encouragement.

Personal networks are built by natural associations, not contrived ones. You might like to think that the CEO of your company is a part of your personal network, but this is not likely to be. But friends within your company, employees at non-competitive companies, trade association employees, community leaders can all be important links in your personal promotion efforts.

The key is reciprocity. If your only role in your personal network is to solicit assistance from your associates they will quickly lose interest in you. They have their own problems, ambitions and needs. You must demonstrate that you can play a role in helping them achieve their objectives.

Chapter 5

External Targets
For Promotional Focus

Simply focusing on internal targets is too limited a promotional focus for your personal promotion plan. All opportunities are not contained within your current position. And even internal opportunities can be influenced by figures outside your company. An effective personal promotion plan requires that you define these external targets and include appropriate strategies to approach them.

Your Customers

Certainly the most important targets for effective contact focus are the customers that your company has placed in your charge. These "customers" can be clients, vendors, fellow employees that you serve, or persons in the community. Your "customers " are those people for which you have primary responsibility. By far, the most important service you can offer your customer is *ready access.*

You are part of *their* support system. You are part of the tools they require for success in *their* positions. Their performance is partially judged by how well they employ what you have to offer.

They also have the right to expect that you will occasionally contribute new ideas to their enterprise. Do you see other solutions within the industry that might be applied in your customers' operations? Are there services your company offers that will provide improved value to your customers?

Customers must see you make their goals, your goals. To do this you need a clear understanding of the organizational structure and dynamics within your customers' organizations. What are the budgeting periods within their organization? What are the internal relationships that affect your customer? What new initiatives do they have underway for which you might make a contribution?

Satisfied customers are the lifeblood of your company's success. Consequently, they are the lifeblood of your career success.

Your personal promotional tools among your customers are largely operational. However, this does not mean they cannot be effectively done and made consistent with your career objectives.

Action reports, conference reports, memos, and special reports are all operational tools that can jointly serve as promotional tools for your career. Don't view them as an operational burden. See them for what they can be – *promotional tools* to demonstrate your value to your customer and to your company.

Prospects

In many ways prospects can be regarded the same as customers. They have the same needs, motivations, and the same resources. A prospect is just a customer that requires additional education.

The key difference is that your relationship is not likely to be as close as that with a customer, and you will have less access to the internal workings of the prospect's company. There is still necessary and available information to be gained about the prospect.

Who are their current suppliers and how were they selected? Who are the gatekeepers and decision-makers within the company? What are the most critical products and services that they buy from outside vendors?

Many of your personal promotional tools will apply to your prospects. There is no reason the "Convention Correspondent" that was described earlier cannot include prospects in the distribution of your convention reports. Perhaps the "white papers" you have created on new industry initiatives can be shared with prospects as well.

> **Prospects must be included in your personal promotional efforts. Not only because they may have access or information about opportunities outside your company, but also because they will become a part of your success when you convert them to customers.**

Career Contemporaries

In many ways, business associates outside your company are the most objective resources you have available. Generally you are in competition with them only in the most peripheral way. They may share common problems with you and can assist you in providing solutions.

They are a conduit for competitive and industry information that may help you in your career. They can provide support that may not be available from your family and co-workers.

Your role in their promotional plan is to ensure that you provide them with whatever assistance you can, and hope that they will reciprocate by sharing information that is of mutual interest and value.

Headhunters

It is the fantasy of every business executive to receive an unexpected call from an important headhunter, offering a lucrative and important position. The line between a headhunter and an employment agency is a fuzzy one and primarily governed by the level at which you are working in the executive pyramid. In any case, anyone who has the ability to help you progress in your career is an important ally.

> **The problem with headhunters is that they are rarely interested in any "head" that is volunteered to them.**

The most important headhunter jobs are always searches that have been commissioned by the employer. The primary responsibility of the headhunter is always to their client -- your prospective employer.

While it is possible to publicize your career directly to headhunters, it is rarely a productive effort. Headhunters are inundated with unsolicited resumes and job seekers. It is easy to see that there is a very low probability that you will be just the right candidate, for the specific jobs they are trying to fill, and that you will happen to submit an unsolicited resume, at just the right time.

This does not mean that headhunters do not aggressively seek candidates. They do so by being aware of what is going on within the industry. They observe who is quoted in industry publications. They measure people they meet at industry gatherings. They read industry publications for executives who have taken the trouble to publish their ideas.

Once a relationship has been established with the headhunter, you should always try to maintain this relationship as long as possible. Keep the headhunter advised of changes in your career. Send non-confidential information that you may have prepared to the headhunter as examples of your work. Recommend friends and co-workers to the headhunter when they are seeking candidates for the jobs you cannot fill.

While any professional friend is valuable, there's no one more valuable than a headhunter with a portfolio of lucrative positions to fill.

Trade And Professional Associations

Every industry supports one or more trade associations to provide education, community and representation to the public and to governing and regulatory bodies. These associations can be as small as a few administrative employees, and as large as the giant Washington-based associations for major industries.

Trade associations provide opportunities to not only expand your skills through their educational programs but also to meet people outside your company who have similar interests to yours and who may provide promotion opportunities. In addition, the trade association staff will actually welcome your interest. The dilemma for trade association officials is simple.

Everyone wants to be recognized. No one wants to work.

Trade associations are filled with unpaid committees and groups that have been charged with reaching some objective. The leaders of these committees may get most of the glory but there's ample opportunity to demonstrate your talents and skills by being a working member of the group.

Trade association staffs are often charged with the responsibility of extracting meaningful results from these committees. Unfortunately this is a case of having responsibility without authority. They will not soon forget any person that provides meaningful assistance to help them achieve a measure of success.

While their role in providing access to new opportunities may not be as direct as that of a headhunter, they can provide broad exposure to other people in the industry.

Meeting The Media And Benefiting From The Experience

It would seem that mass media reporters would be obvious targets for your personal promotion efforts. However, this is rarely the case. Not only are general news media largely indifferent to business activities, they are even less interested in the activities of an individual executive within a company.

Unless you commit embezzlement, are charged with sexual harassment, or get hit by a car in the company parking lot, your business activities and ambitions are not likely to be of much interest to the general press.

This does not mean that there are not opportunities for utilizing the general press in your personal promotion plans. You simply have to direct your activities into areas of interest to them. The most readily available avenue is your work with local community efforts. Reporting on activities for the betterment of the community is the natural news beat for local media. Once again, if you can demonstrate leadership to the community in these activities, and this is reported in the local press, this will be noticed by your company's management.

An easier target for your promotion activities is a news representative from *trade* media. These are publications that have a specific interest in the industry in which you work.

While they might not be interested in you as an individual, they have a keen interest in any significant activities within the industry. Your company, depending upon its size or ability to innovate, can be an important interest to one of these representatives.

Trade news is not often as exciting as general news. Consequently, you may find that trade news reporters are particularly responsive to any type of originality you can suggest in approaching industry news. New products, new techniques, new organizations and new ways of doing things are all things of particular interest to the trade reporter.

In addition, it is sometime difficult for trade news reporters to find creditable sources for their news reports. Most companies do not go out of their way to publicize which of their employees is involved in specific activities.

Once you become a part of the contact list of a trade media reporter, you may find yourself called about all kinds of subjects and events, as these reporters seek to find resources within your industry. These contacts can provide additional avenues for you to obtain visibility within the industry and your company.

Once you have established a relationship with any reporter, they become fair targets for the various personal promotion tools and techniques that you will employ.

It is not that reporters will not understand that your promotional efforts are largely self-serving, it is just that they understand and accept this symbiotic relationship between reporters and their sources.

Whether you are dealing with trade media or general news media, one rule you must follow in your personal promotion efforts is this: respond immediately. Regardless of whether their publication schedules are daily or monthly, all reporters are working on a fixed timeline. A response that is delayed may be a response that is worthless to the reporter.

It's not possible to buy your way into legitimate media of any type. But there is a currency that is valued and which will be accepted:

- ☑ Be helpful
- ☑ Be interesting
- ☑ Be newsworthy
- ☑ *Be responsive.*

Chapter 6

Essential Skills For A Successful Personal Promotion Plan

While the primary focus within these pages is suggesting and describing the tools and techniques that create a successful plan, a critical element must come from within.

> **You must have the <u>will</u> and the ambition to be a success in order to make it happen.**

It has long been recognized that most successful *entrepreneurs* have an almost indomitable will for success and that this quality keeps them driving toward their goals. They will make whatever sacrifices are necessary, they will focus on what is necessary for success, and they will recognize no barriers that may appear in their way. While these may not be particularly admirable personal qualities, they are important ones for business success.

Some degree of this ambition and intensity must be present in you or the quality and effectiveness of your personal promotion plan is likely to be limited.

In addition to personal will, one of the most important talents you can acquire is effective writing and speaking skills.

> **A key goal of your personal promotion plan is to ensure your favorable visibility within your organization. One readily available avenue to accomplish this is to become known for the quality of your written and verbal communications.**

Communication Skills

It could be said that all promotion is nothing but an *organized* form of persuasion. Examples can be seen throughout business promotional activities.

> **Advertising is an attempt to attract attention to a product. Marketing is an attempt to effectively manage a company's communication efforts. A personal promotion plan is an attempt to persuade people of your value to their enterprise, by achieving greater visibility.**

The communication skills you possess are critical tools for the success of your plan. Fortunately, communication skills are readily acquired should you have deficiencies.

An essential first element in any communication is vocabulary. Ideally, your education and industry experience will have created a broad vocabulary that you can effectively employ in your personal promotional efforts. However, this is sometimes not the case.

It has little to do with intelligence. It may have little to do with education. Our colleges are increasingly graduating students with a very narrow focus. They may be experts in engineering or medicine or science or computers, but they don't have the requisite skills to present their ideas to the world.

If you see that your communication skills are not what they should be, immediately take steps to improve them.

Buying a book to build your vocabulary may have somewhat of a humiliating feel to it after you have graduated from college and perhaps even achieved a degree of business success. However, it is a simple act that can greatly expand your ability to express yourself.

An interesting thing about acquiring new words is that once they are in your mind they seem to beg to be used. No one should employ complicated words when simple ones will suffice, but you will find that relevant thoughts you have may be easier to express once you have found the appropriate vocabulary.

Personal Presentation Skills

Effectively presenting to a group, large or small, is a necessary skill for any successful executive. Since many people so dislike doing it, the person that does it well will be especially noticed. Presentation skills are important to the *successful executive*. They are even more important to the *successful leader*.

The best way to acquire presentation skills is just to make presentations. Begin with your friends; progress to your co-workers; succeed with your bosses.

For good or bad, Microsoft PowerPoint® has become the essential tool of business presentations. Using this program well has value both as a tool for personal promotion, and also as a business resource you can build and refine.

A personal library of PowerPoint slides may be the tool that allows you to quickly develop effective presentations, in times of crisis, with a minimum amount time, while your competition is still attempting to get organized. In addition, senior executives consider effective presentation skills as one mark of potential candidates for promotion.

Follow the ten easy steps described below and you are guaranteed to be better that 95% of all the presentations you will see this year:

☑ **Only mice can read mouse type** - The single most common mistake made with presentations is cramming too much information on a slide, thereby making the *point size* (height of the letters) too small.

Of course, *you* can read it. You're standing at the front of the room. However, you're objective is to have the person sitting in the back of the room be able to read it.

The "default" point sizes offered by PowerPoint and other presentation programs will allow approximately six lines, of approximately six words each, per slide. Change these standards at the peril of your presentation. If you must present more information than will fit on a single slide, create additional slides with a common heading.

☑ **Present. DON'T READ.** - If your contribution is to stand in front of your audience and read your slides, don't go. Just mail the slides to the audience. It's cheaper. The points on your slides should emphasize and support what you have to say. If you begin each new point by reading it from the slide, it will appear that the information is as much a surprise to you as it is to your audience.

☑ **A presentation is (wo)man + machine** - A "presentation" is NOT a collection of slides.

It should be the combination of the presenter's persuasive words, the presenter's presence, and the visual support provided by the slides.

It is highly unlikely that your bulleted slides will be that impressive to the audience. If your presentation is to be memorable, YOU have to be the memorable part. The best way to ensure what you say is memorable is to allow plenty of time to prepare and practice, practice, practice.

☑ **Leave behind something besides your memory** - Your spoken words and your projected slides are transitory. No one in your audience will be able to remember all that you say.

ALWAYS have a "leave behind" for the audience. This should not be a copy of your presentation. If you presented it properly, they don't need to read it. Leave a summary. Leave the five key points. Leave the next action steps. Leave the contract.

☑ **Customize the collateral** - Printed collateral material is an important sales tool. It represents corporate promises. It gives a professional shell to your material.

However, it doesn't include your prospect's name. Promises you type may be much more powerful. Your brochures will say, "Our clients can expect . . ."; you can say, "Acme Industries can expect . . .." Which phrase do you think Acme is likely to find more interesting?

☑ **Spreadsheets belong on paper** - First,
NEVER project a spreadsheet. Second, Third
and Fourth, NEVER project a spreadsheet.
All those numbers and columns and totals
may contain a wealth of important
information, but when you project a
spreadsheet your audience will most likely
just laugh at your presumption that anyone
can read it.

Generally, all those spreadsheet numbers
lead to only one or two conclusions.
Present the conclusions. Pass out copies of
the spreadsheets.

☑ **Line & staff charts** - See "Spreadsheets."

☑ **Three points and you're out** - Your
presentation will be only a small part of the
avalanche of information that your audience
will receive this week. Your presentation
must penetrate an audience's skepticism,
fatigue, boredom and information overload.

It is presumptuous for you to believe that
you can do this with 10-15 points. Focus on
3-5 points that are essential for the success
of your presentation.

Begin by telling your audience the points
you intend to make; make your points as
persuasively as possible; restate your points
and conclusions at the end of your
presentation. Take questions. Sit down.

☑ **Even clipart is worth a thousand words** -
Photographs are generally best to illustrate
your presentation but may not be available.

However, line art or "clipart" is readily available to you. Clipart is designed by professional artists to illustrate *concepts*. For this reason alone, clipart sometimes can be more useful than photographs.

A modest library of clipart is standard with PowerPoint. Use it only if you must. It is likely to be well known to the members of your audience. Invest $40 at your local software store and you can get a library of 25,000 pieces of clipart to add visual power to your words.

☑ **Relax. It will all be over in 20 minutes -** It's well known that many people dread speaking in front of an audience. You may never be completely comfortable in presentations. Don't worry. You don't have to be comfortable to be successful – only *professional.* Your audience will not expect you to be an entertainer. Just don't bore them. Don't waste their time. And, **DON'T READ YOUR SLIDES!**

How To Make A Presentation To Your President

Even experienced presenters are often nervous when they have to make a presentation to a very senior executive. They know that senior executives are experts at being the "presentee" and they will no doubt judge your performance against others they have heard.

However, if they didn't want to hear what you have to say, you wouldn't be invited to speak. In addition, if you didn't know more about the subject than anyone in the room, you probably wouldn't be there.

Consider these points the next time you have to make an executive presentation:

- ☑ Presenting to **senior executives** is a matter of economy, efficiency and strategy.

- ☑ Always begin by **reviewing** what you plan to present with the audience. Maybe it's not what the President is expecting to hear.

- ☑ Once the most senior person in the audience agrees with your agenda, you have an implied "**buy-in**" for your presentation, and that includes the necessary time to fairly present it.

- ☑ Never hand out your **written proposal** until after your presentation. (You did prepare a written proposal didn't you?) Otherwise, you'll just be presenting to their down-turned heads.

- ☑ Forget the **jokes.** The President may not share your sense of humor. Besides, are you making a serious proposal or doing a standup routine?

- ☑ Maintain **eye contact** with the people in your audience whose approval is most important to your proposal.

- ☑ **Summarize**, don't itemize. Unless you think the President doubts your honesty, don't review your research. Present significant and unexpected information. Present

conclusions. Present recommendations.
Present action plans.

☑ Never let your **passion** for the subject
overwhelm the rationality of your
arguments. The President is there to hear
an objective presentation.

☑ Deal with "**snipers**" immediately. If
someone in the audience begins to squirm,
grimace and generally indicate their
disagreement with your positions, stop the
presentation. Turn the focus on them.
Politely ask to what they are objecting.
Snipers are rarely as prepared as you to
present arguments. They likely will become
quieter, but you can expect to have to deal
with their opposition at a later time.

☑ Always **restate** a question to be sure you
understand it and that others heard it.

☑ Never respond to objections with
provocative questions (i.e. "Can't you
understand what will happen if we don't
implement this proposal?!") You are there
to present information, not arguments.
Besides, even if you win an argument with
your President, you lose.

☑ If questioners ask a question that turns into
a **competing speech**, be polite but return
the discussion to the key points made by
your presentation.

☑ Unless you have total rejection of your
proposal, always get **agreement** on a next,
tangible action – even if it is only to let you
continue to pursue your investigation.

The 10-Minute Presentation

The importance of presentation skills to demonstrate your skills, your thinking, and your confidence cannot be over emphasized. Any time invested in polishing your words, your presentation tools and your presentation manner is time well spent.

You hope to deliver perfection with any presentation. But what if attaining such a standard is not possible. Suppose circumstances won't allow perfection.

What if you are told to present a ten-minute update to your company's Executive Committee on your current project? And -- you go on in ten minutes.

This is a common demand when executives meet. Perhaps they have been called upon to make a decision and find they don't have the information they need. *You* are going to provide the needed information.

Impromptu presentations are an everyday part of an executive's life. There is no reason you should be spared. *Impromptu presentations* may be even more valuable in demonstrating your skills than *formal presentations.* You have the opportunity to not only present the quality of your thinking, but also your presence and poise in a stressful situation.

Impromptu presentations also demand brevity and conciseness, qualities that are always appreciated by executives in subordinates.

You can survive impromptu presentations. You can even use them to your advantage. Follow these easy steps the next time the opportunity arises:

☑ **Rationalize** – Take the first 30 seconds of your available time to calm yourself and accept that you have only been asked to give a brief presentation – not an inaugural address.

☑ **Minimize** – You must limit your presentation to only the most important points – generally three to five.

☑ **Organize** – A good structure is Background, Challenges, Proposed Actions, and Benefits.

☑ **Presence** – For personal promotion purposes, an effective presence is equally important as the quality of your presentation content. The image you want to demonstrate is *casual* (consistent with the spontaneity of your invitation) and *confident* (reflecting the skills that you bring to your responsibilities).

☑ **Practice** – As you work on projects, periodically imagine that you have been asked to give a ten-minute presentation. Practice the steps outlined above. Not only will the practice improve your presentation skills, it may help you keep your focus. If you find you can't adequately deliver a "ten

minute presentation," perhaps your
project's objectives need more refinement.

Writing Skills

The single most important skill you can acquire in business is the ability to clearly express yourself in writing. (Go back and read the preceding sentence five more times.)

The ability to express yourself, clearly and succinctly, in memos, E-mails, bulletins, and presentations should be one of your most important ambitions.

The quality of writing in business today is abysmal. You can achieve distinction simply by doing a competent job.

Effective Writing, Step By Step

☑ **Start with an outline.** That's right just like they tried to teach you in elementary school. An outline forms the trunk and branches of your written document. (Some people complain that starting with an outline interferes with just "getting to the writing." Yes, it probably will -- for the betterment of your final document.)

An outline is just a plan for writing. You can change it just readily as anything else you write. The benefits are the same as when they tried to teach you to use one in school: it helps you organize your thoughts, it exposes weaknesses in your arguments and it gives you a roadmap of what to write next.

☑ **Follow military rules.** The largest training organization in this country is no college you know. It's the U.S. military. They have had to develop training systems that impart knowledge to people from all walks of life, and who probably are also tired and disinterested in the subject matter.

Military training is built on three rules: Tell 'em what you are going to tell 'em; then tell 'em; then tell 'em what you told 'em.

If you learn nothing else about writing, you probably can get by with just those three rules.

☑ **Write for the one person** that you most want to convince. "Carbon copies" are an accepted part of business writing (even though you probably couldn't find a real piece of carbon paper in your office if I offered you $100 for it.)

You probably know when you write a document that more than one person will receive it. But, good writing will never be written for a group. You will make too many compromises and offer too many arguments.

There is generally one recipient that is most important to the acceptance of your arguments. Keep that person in mind. Think of their sensitivities and interests. Pretend you are making an oral presentation to them as you write.

☑ **Telegraph your punches.** Regardless of how well you do it or how important it is to you, your recipients will likely see reading your document as a chore. They read John Gresham's words for fun. Yours they will read because they feel they must.

Consequently, the fiction writer's tricks of misdirection, surprise, and mystery are not for you. Your job is to do everything you can to make the reader's task as easy as possible. Using the Military Rules described above are a good start.

But also think about the sequence of your arguments so that they will form a logical structure to reach your conclusions. Use transitions that help your reader move from one argument to the next. Don't *reveal* your conclusions; make them *inevitable* after your arguments are presented.

☑ **Write hot. Edit cold.** Passion may seem a strange quality to try to introduce into business writing, but it can be a powerful tool. Writing in the heat of a passionate belief can uncover ideas you didn't know you had and arguments you had not formed. It can give you energy to write more than you intended. Even if you cannot generate passion for the subject matter of your document, perhaps you can generate passion about convincing the reader of the correctness of your position.

Editing requires an entirely different approach. If possible, it is always better to let your words rest for a few days before editing them for corrections and improvements. When your arguments are too fresh in your head, you will find that your brain may make corrections to your words that your eyes don't actually see.

Even better, find a qualified, disinterested party to review your document for you. They can more readily spot typos, poor sentence structure and weak arguments.

Start With A Template

In word processing, presentation and spreadsheet programs, there is a powerful device known as a *template.* A template is simply a digital file that allows you to achieve more productivity by not "reinventing the wheel" with repetitive tasks.

In communications, an outline, a previously prepared similar document, or a tightly structured form, typically represent the "template." In the discussion of basic correspondence that follows, the objective should always be to develop an effective template.

A template is not rigid and unchanging. It is improved as you find better solutions or get better at your craft.

As important as knowing *how* to put things in writing, is knowing *when* to put things in writing. Exhibit 6A can help you make that decision.

Exhibit 6A: When You Should Put It In Writing

- ☑ Did the matter you discussed involve significant amounts of time and\or money?
- ☑ Did you discuss significant changes to the customary way of doing things?
- ☑ Do you need to advise others of what was discussed by sending copies of the meeting notes?
- ☑ Were significant tasks assigned to the people that met, or to people not present at the meeting?
- ☑ Are you uncertain whether the participants in the meeting reached a consensus about the points discussed in the meeting?

A Professional Resume Upon Demand

Everyone who has sought a desirable job has had to prepare a professional resume. New professional resumes are generally prepared each time you seek a new position. They *should be* customized for each specific position you apply for.

The resume is your "calling card" in the employment industry. It is both a basic tool for success and one that can be made increasingly effective as you achieve success with your personal promotion plan.

You should always have a complete and up-to-date professional resume in your files. You may not have time to update it when an important opportunity arises. You may find that just the effort to update your resume will suggest specific weaknesses or strengths in your personal promotion plan that should be addressed.

In addition, to a professional resume, perhaps you also should begin to develop a *professional vitae.*

Professional Vitae

Those in the academic world have long utilized a very lengthy form of resume called *curriculum vitae.* This is a detailed account of the academic's professional and personal activities over an entire career: the longer the career, the longer the document.

This can be a very effective tool for the professional as well as the academic. While there are few employers that would accept a resume of this length, it can provide a detailed record of your professional activities that will be useful throughout your professional career.

Memory fails, details are lost, but the facts you record in your professional vitae are constant. It can document activities that may be of interest to future employers as well as jog your own memory about

skills that you have used in the past. Exhibit 6B
describes the type of information you should include
in your Professional Vitae.

In additional to personal information about you,
there are certain documents and correspondence that
you will be called upon to present throughout your
career. Producing these documents well is simply
another way to promote your career within an
organization.

Exhibit 6B: Outline for Professional Vitae

Biographical Data
- ☑ Birthdate
- ☑ Place of Birth
- ☑ Citizenship

Education
- ☑ Your highest post-graduate degree, year degree received
- ☑ Name of degree granting institution
- ☑ Specialization: degree specialization or major
- ☑ Minor: degree minor, if relevant

- ☑ Bachelor of Arts/Science, year degree received
- ☑ Name of degree granting institution
- ☑ Major: major field of study
- ☑ Major: second major field of study, if relevant
- ☑ GPA: undergraduate GPA, if relevant

Relevant Additional Graduate Coursework
☑ Topic or specialty 1
  Course 1
  Course 2
  Course 3

☑ Topic or specialty 2
  Course 1
  Course 2
  Course 3

Honors and Awards
☑ First honor or award

☑ Second honor or award

☑ Third honor or award

Work Experience
☑ First job title – such as Sales Representative

☑ Qualifying information such as "Data Processing Sales"

☑ Company, date started-date ended

☑ Supervisor: supervisor's name

☑ Job duties

☑ Second job title

☑ Qualifying information

☑ Company name, date started-date ended

☑ Supervisor: supervisor's name

☑ Job duties

Publications
☑ Topic 1 – publication 1

☑ Topic 2 - publication 2

Conferences\Seminars\Training

☑ Conference 1 – Conference primary subject – Conference dates

☑ Conference 2 – Conference primary subject – Conference dates

---

Conference\Seminar Presentations

☑ Conference 1 – Conference primary subject – Conference dates – Presentation topic

☑ Conference 2 – Conference primary subject – Conference dates – Presentation topic

---

Relevant Computer Experience

☑ Program 1, Program 2

Relevant Professional Training\Coursework

☑ Topic or specialty 1
　　Course 1
　　Course 2
　　Course 3

☑ Topic or specialty 2
　　Course 1
　　Course 2
　　Course 3

Professional Service and Volunteer Work

☑ Service event 1 title - description of service episode 1.

☑ Service event 2 title - description of service episode 2.

Professional References

☑ 1st reference name – company name, company address, telephone number, E-mail address

☑ 2nd reference name – company name, company address, telephone number, E-mail address

☑ 3rd reference name – company name, company address, telephone number, E-mail address

---

Proposals

A proposal may be something as complicated as an entire new enterprise or as simple as justification for buying a new piece of business equipment. It includes research, analysis and conclusions. If your company has not established a corporate format for proposals, Exhibit 6C will give you a start.

Exhibit 6C: Outline for a Project Proposal

☑ Executive summary

☑ General description of project

☑ Project objectives

☑ Value of project to Company

☑ Relationship of project to other company activities

☑ Company strengths & weaknesses in this area

☑ Competitive analysis

☑ Significant risks and opportunities

☑ Required technology

☑ Measurement standards
☑ Budget and resources required
☑ Staff and management of project
☑ Timelines for project

Status Report

Many executives require the submission of a weekly or monthly status report from those that directly report to them. You not only should embrace this requirement, you should demand it. It is your personal newsletter to your boss. You are both the writer and the editor of this information. It will provide you opportunities to offer both expanded information on your successes and mitigating information on your failures.

Even better, perhaps your boss's boss will come to see the value of copies of your status report coming directly to him\her.

When this happens you have a direct, approved avenue of communication with the person most likely to produce opportunities for your next promotion.

☑ **Exhibit 6D: Outline for a Status Report**

☑ An **Executive Summary** of your Report

☑ Itemization of **projects\key activities** that occupied your time during the period on which you are reporting, and the **results** that were achieved

☑ **Assistance** needed from your supervisor to accomplish your responsibilities

☑ Additional **resources** that you need

☑ Your **objectives** for the next time period

Conference Report

The *conference or action report* is an essential tool in many fields of business: Advertising agencies, sales departments, lawyers, consultants, etc. It should be more widely used.

It provides a record of meetings, telephones calls and any other encounters in which important decisions are made. It outlines what was discussed; it summarizes positions expressed; and, it identifies parties from whom action is expected.

It is both a working tool and an important record should there be disputes about what has transpired. Your ability to effectively summarize the content of a meeting with clients, executives or co-workers will not go unnoticed and will provide another tool to demonstrate to your management your talents and abilities. The outline shown in Exhibit 6E is commonly used in may Conference Reports.

Agenda

Perform a public service. The next meeting you host, create a written agenda; distribute it in advance; report the meeting results.

Agenda-less meetings waste more corporate time and talents than all the baseball pools, office romances and water cooler discussions combined.

Exhibit 6E: Outline for a Conference Report

☑ Date and Place of the conference\meeting
☑ Purpose of the conference
☑ Names of participants attending the conference
☑ Itemization of each subject discussed
  -- *Background information on the subject*
  -- *Status of the subject before the meeting*
  -- *Summary of the individual comments made*
    on the subject by participants in the meeting
  -- *Description of any consensus reached*
    by the group about the subject
  -- *Actions assigned to individuals the subject*
☑ Date of any planned future meetings

One insightful manager has suggested that all company meetings be conducted standing up. In this way, people would focus on the objectives at hand and not on posturing, demonstrating their misunderstandings and generally wasting their co-workers time. All too often, the only significant decision reached in a meeting is the date of the next meeting. Use the information provided in Exhibit 6F as a guide.

When the meeting is over, provide a written summary of what has transpired. Requirements for meeting notes are generally the same as the conference report described above: an itemization of what was discussed; an interpretation of the comments that were offered; and the person's responsible for the actions selected.

Exhibit 6F: Outline For Meeting Agenda\Report

- ☑ Title\Purpose of meeting
- ☑ Date of meeting
- ☑ Place of meeting
- ☑ Moderator for meeting
- ☑ List of Attendees
- ☑ Purpose of meeting
- ☑ Specific objectives for meeting
- ☑ Background information for meeting (may be attached as exhibit)
- ☑ Summary of results from past meetings on subject

☑ Key topic(s) to be considered at meeting and
name of person assigned to lead discussion of
topic in meeting. For each topic record and
publish:

-- Defined topic problem\opportunity
-- Importance\priority of topic
-- Key comments made in the discussion
   on the topic
-- Suggested solutions
-- Additional information required
-- Schedule of key events
-- Defined action to be taken and person(s)
assigned

☑ Date of any future meeting

E-mails

E-mails are strange bits of communication. They
are everywhere. They arrive throughout the day. And
all too often, they are casually prepared. E-mails offer
you the opportunity to communicate with hundreds of
people by a single keystroke. Unfortunately, they also
carry the opportunity to make a fool of you in front of
hundreds of people -- with this same keystroke.

Because E-mails can be so easily prepared, few people take seriously their preparation. However, E-mails are rapidly replacing the corporate memo. They deserve the same care and thoughtfulness as any other important corporate communication.

One valuable aspect of the E-mail culture to personal promotion is a certain loosening of strictures in broadcasting information beyond your immediate supervisor. Because the act seems so casual, there seems to be broader acceptance of distributing your words to broader groups.

In personal promotion, it is natural that you will elect to include in this broader E-mail group those individuals that are important for your personal success.

If you are going to effectively employ this new tool, you need to use it with care. Exhibit 6G offers some ideas to ensure that the arrival of your E-mails is welcomed, rather than dreaded.

Exhibit 6G: Best Practices For E-mail

☑ Regardless of the number of people that will receive your E-mail, write your message as if you were speaking to only **one person**.

☑ Always remember that E-mail systems make it easy for the recipient to **forward** your E-mail to one or more people. Are you prepared for your words to be read by more than the original recipient?

☑ Use whatever **formatting** tools your E-mail system offers to make your message easier to read – bullets, indents, bold, italic, underline, color.

☑ Never write in **all caps**. IT LOOKS LIKE YOU ARE SCREAMING AT THE READER.

☑ Most people find words on video monitors to be harder to read than words on paper. Use at least a **12-point** typeface.

☑ Don't send big, dense blocks of copy. Break up your paragraphs. **Paragraph breaks** don't cost any extra.

Writing Internal Corporate Bulletins

The internal corporate bulletin is the key communication document for the distribution of information about major programs and changes. It may also be designed for distribution to distributors, customers and vendors.

It is generally much longer than a Memo and more broadly distributed. Since it is so broadly distributed the problems arising from erroneous or poorly written bulletins are magnified.

Within many companies, the style and content of bulletins can vary widely. A wise company standard is that a single style of internal bulletin be adopted, not because it is inherently *superior* to those used in the past, but because it is *predictable.*

An internal bulletin is not an exercise in creative writing but a tool to transfer the maximum amount of information as painlessly and efficiently as possible. The reader should be allowed to apply knowledge and techniques learned in reading past bulletins to understanding of the information in a new current bulletin.

It your company hasn't established a standard for company bulletins, be an innovator. Adopt the standards described in Exhibit 6H.

Writing A Marketing Plan

A marketing plan is often confused with a corporate plan. It should be a part of any corporate plan, but a corporate plan is likely to be closely tied to a company's fiscal year, while marketing plans may have to be made, revised, discarded, and replicated throughout the year.

Exhibit 6H: Best Practices For Internal Bulletins:

☑ Avoid sending lengthy bulletins by *E-mail.*

☑ Information should be presented in an order from the most *general* to the most *specific.* Think like a newspaper reporter.

☑ The *body* of the bulletin should be used to give an overall picture of the subject.

☑ *Exhibits* should be used for highly detailed\specific materials.

☑ *Advantages* of exhibits:

-- Can be used as reference documents
   by the recipient.
-- Separates information that may be of interest
   to only some of the recipients.
-- By segregating the specific details, it is easier
   for the reader to follow overall presentation.
-- Can easily accommodate information that is
   best presented in differing formats.

☑ *Refer* to the appropriate exhibits at the appropriate point in the body of the Bulletin.

☑ Always *attach* the exhibits in the order in which they are referenced in the body of the bulletin.

☑ Use paragraphs of no more than five sentences. *Short sentences* are generally better. Don't exhaust your reader requiring that they fight their way through dense prose.

☑ *Avoid horizontal* ("landscape ") pages if possible.

☑ *Avoid "legal"* size pages. They don't file well.

☑ Avoid using a **presentation program** to write "memos." It increases the paper bulk with no communication advantage.

☑ Make use of **organization and emphasis** techniques commonly available in standard word processing programs: Bullet points, italic, bold face, different point sizes (no more than three in body copy), indentation, etc.

☑ Use points of **emphasis** judiciously. Don't continuously SCREAM at the reader.

☑ Review your bulletin for *"scanability."* Reading corporate bulletins is a responsibility, not a recreation. Help the reader find pertinent points quickly.

☑ Always have a co-worker, not familiar with the subject matter, **review your bulletin** to test your communication efforts.

☑ Always keep in mind that while your bulletin may be of critical importance to you, the recipient may view it as just another task that must be **understood, communicated to subordinates, and executed.**

While few people may ever have the sole responsibility of writing a corporate plan, most people who want to progress in a company should know how to write marketing plans. While marketing plans have to be specifically tailored to a company's needs, opportunities, resources and situation, Exhibit 6I suggests a way for you to start this task.

Exhibit 6I: Outline For Marketing Plan

Title
- ☑ Descriptive Information
- ☑ Date of presentation
- ☑ Names of persons responsible for plan

Plan Objectives & Strategies
- ☑ What do you hope to accomplish
- ☑ What will change as a result of the successful execution of the plan
- ☑ What are the benefits to the company

Market Summary
- ☑ Past, Present, & Future
- ☑ Review changes in market share, leadership, players, market shifts, costs, pricing, competition

Product Definition
- ☑ Describe product/service being marketed

Competition
- ☑ Review the competitive landscape
- ☑ Provide an overview of product competitors, their strengths and weaknesses
- ☑ Position each competitor's product against the new product or service

Positioning
- ☑ Describe how you expect the target customer to position the product or service among their choices
- ☑ Prepare a statement that distinctly defines the product in its market and against its competition over time
- ☑ Describe how this position will benefit the company

Consumer Promise
- ☑ Statement summarizing the benefit of the product or service to the consumer

Communication Strategies
- ☑ Messages to be delivered to each audience
- ☑ Themes that will be present throughout the communication efforts

Target Consumer Demographics
- ☑ Describe target by all relevant variables

Packaging & fulfillment
- ☑ Description\illustration of product packaging
- ☑ Discuss form, pricing, look, strategy
- ☑ Discuss fulfillment issues for items not shipped directly with product

Cost Of Goods
- ☑ Summarize Cost of Goods and Bill of Materials

Launch Strategies
- ☑ Launch plan if time of launch is significant for product's success

Promotion Budget
- ☑ Supply back up material with detailed budget information for review
- ☑ Provide context for promotion budget by describing other plans or competitive efforts

Public Relations
- ☑ Strategy & execution
- ☑ PR plan highlights, including editorial calendars, speaking engagements, conference schedules, etc.

Advertising
- ☑ Overview of communication strategy
- ☑ Introduce key advertising themes and creative concepts
- ☑ Overview of media, timing, ad spending

Direct Marketing
- ☑ Overview of strategy, vehicles & timing
- ☑ Overview of response targets, goals & budget

Third-Party Marketing
- ☑ Co-marketing arrangements with other companies

Pricing
- ☑ Summarize specific pricing or pricing strategies
- ☑ Compare to similar products
- ☑ Summarize policy relevant to key pricing issues

Distribution
- ☑ Summarize channels of distribution
- ☑ Specific distribution by channel
- ☑ Show what share of distribution will be contributed by each channel
- ☑ Vertical Markets\Segments\Opportunities
- ☑ Address distribution strategies for each market or segment
- ☑ Address use of third-party partners in distribution to vertical markets
- ☑ Describe promotional efforts for each distribution channel

International
- ☑ Discuss issues specific to international distribution
- ☑ Rationalize promotional strategies and themes with international sensitivities
- ☑ International pricing strategy
- ☑ Localization issues & local product variations

Success Metrics
- ☑ First year goals & additional year(s) goals
- ☑ Measures of success/failure
- ☑ Requirements for success
- ☑ Isolate review points that are critical to success

How To Work A Room\Build A Network

Today, it's called "Networking." It used to be called "working a room." Nothing has really changed. It's always been about meeting and knowing the people you want to know. It seems like some people are born doing it well. However, Mr. Keillor's "shy people" as well as most of the rest of us have to learn this skill.

We want people to like and respect us. Most of all we want not to be embarrassed by rejection! Moreover, our mothers taught us to be modest and not push ourselves on other people. Once again, Mom's well-intentioned advice may be inhibiting you from doing what you need to do to promote yourself.

It's not that networking is necessarily going to find a new "best friend" for you. That's not the standard. You want people to know you and your talents and your interests. You need to know *their* talents and interests if you are to help them and be able to form a mutually rewarding relationship.

Your objective is not just to make a new acquaintance at a meeting. Your objective is to build a relationship that will last after the meeting is over.

You may find that the people you meet will be willing partners in your efforts. Just as you hope they will become a valuable part of your professional circle, you are giving them the opportunity to include you and your talents in their circle.

The reality is that most of the people you don't know also want to know more people. They may be just as hesitant as you to make the first move.

So, you take the first step. Show them how to do it. You'll get better at it. You may even come to enjoy the challenge. You'll almost certainly enjoy most of the new people you'll meet.

There is no reason not to approach expanding your circle of contacts in a social situation the same way you would any of the other personal promotion tasks. There are specific things you can do to improve your success in networking:

☑ **Have clear objectives** in mind when you enter a meeting or social gathering. Whom do you want to meet? What do you want to know? What do you want them to know about you? Is there a particular event \ process \ person that you want to know more about?

☑ **Come prepared.** Have you anticipated who you think will be at the meeting? Do you have your business cards? Do you have your personal cards? Do you know three new things that you think people at the meeting might want to know? Do you have something on which you can write notes, names, and addresses?

☑ **What can you do for them?** As you meet people, determine what you might do for the person you are meeting. How can you accommodate them? What service can you provide? It is much better to make a first call after meeting someone to offer to help, rather than to ask for help.

☑ **Follow-up in writing.** In these days of quick telephone calls and poorly written E-mails, receiving even a casually written note can be a memorable event for the recipient.

A written note gives you an opportunity to confirm that you have correctly recorded information about your new acquaintance in your contact file. It also gives you an opportunity to reinforce to the contact *your* name, address, telephone number and interests.

The best thing about learning the skills described in this chapter is that they not only will help you in your business life, but also in your personal life. Who does not want to present themselves well, be more articulate, meet more people, have more adventures?

So, write a letter, send an E-mail, give an impromptu talk, meet a new friend. The rewards far outweigh the risks.

Chapter 7

Personal Promotion Tools

There has never been a better time to be a one-person promotion team. The easy availability of low cost desktop computers and inexpensive printers places powerful communication tools at anyone's disposal.

Your desktop computer is the heart of your personal promotion effort. It's not only the engine that distributes your message; it's a vast storage cabinet, as well as a communication device that will allow you to exchange information from around the world.

The computer is a "mass medium" that you can own. Computers excel at repetition. That's what communicating to more than one person is all about. It allows you to take a single message that might have taken two hours to compose, and thirty minutes to type, and distribute it to hundreds of people within a minute.

Your computer will help you correct your spelling errors, maintain your mailing list, suggest a better use of grammar and manage the personalized printing of paper messages.

Corporate Or Personal Computer

You may already be working with a company-owned computer. One of the first decisions you will face is whether or not to manage your personal promotion plan on your corporate computer or to invest in a personal computer. The obvious advantage to the corporate computer is that it is available to you essentially without cost.

There is some ethical question about using corporate resources for an activity that is partially for personal benefit. However, we have already seen that your company has a vested interest in your doing well, and in your being seen as a successful employee by clients and the community-at-large. In addition, you are unlikely to find any corporate computer system that does not have some small amount of personal use by all employees.

Corporate Or Personal Data

The most serious ethical and legal question you will face about using any corporate resource has to do with *information* such as customer profiles, that you have obtained in the course of your work. You have to consider that your personal promotion effort may

extend beyond your tenure with your current
employer.

**Information about customers and
prospects is an important corporate
asset. Companies will vigorously defend
the confidentiality of this critical
information.**

It is generally accepted that information that is
commonly available in industry directories does not
constitute confidential corporate information. It is
when this information is classified, enhanced with
other company information and graded by such things
as sales volume, etc., that serious questions of
confidentiality arise.

You must determine for yourself what corporate
information is clearly confidential and may only be
used so long as you are an employee of your
company, and that commonly available to all.
Obviously if you are an entrepreneur or the owner of
the company these questions do not arise.

Personal Promotion Hardware

If you decide to use your corporate computer in
your personal promotion efforts, then the decision
about a computer is easy – you use the one you have,
desktop or laptop. If you plan to purchase a new
computer for your work the second question you will
face (after you have determined the budget you can

spend) is *desktop* or *laptop*. Either is suitable for a personal promotion campaign. Either will drive whatever printer you ultimately select.

Fortunately most people these days have sufficient experience with all types of computers to be able to make an informed choice about these two options. However, Exhibit 7A will remind you of the key differences between these two options.

Exhibit 7A: Comparing Desktop And Laptop Computers

Desktop Advantages

☑ Full size keyboard more comfortable

☑ Larger screen easier to read

☑ Many more options available to customize the computer's capabilities

☑ Much larger hard drive capacities are available

☑ Compared to a laptop with equal capabilities, may be 50% to 75% cheaper

Desktop Disadvantages

☑ You can't hold it in your lap

☑ You can't use it on an airplane

☑ You can't move it to the library while you are collecting information

☑ You can't take notes on it in your client's office

☑ It's ugly and takes up a lot of space

Laptop Advantages

☑ It can go wherever you go

☑ Since it's more readily available, you are more likely to put it to good use

☑ It gives you the cool look of an executive, rather than the dreary look of a clerk

---

Laptop Disadvantages

☑ The screen is smaller, dimmer and probably harder to read

☑ As a mobile tool, you are more likely to damage it

☑ It is readily stolen - possibly with your valuable information on its hard drive

☑ If you *can* work at home perhaps your boss *will expect* you to work at home

☑ It's more expensive

Selecting a Printer

If anything, the decision of which printer to select is even more important than which computer. Fortunately, excellent, low-cost printers are available today. You are unlikely to make a serious error. However, there still are important differences between printers available to you.

Inkjet printers are where the action is today. Printer manufacturers have discovered the "razor and razor blade" marketing technique and are practically giving away inkjet printers. They have learned that you will spend more on inkjet refills than you ever did on the purchase price of the printer. In addition, they have so improved the quality of inkjet printers that they are essentially the equals of laser printers in output quality.

Laser printers are the "old men" of personal computer printers. They were revolutionary improvements over old dot-matrix printers because they made it easy to utilize a wide variety of finely crafted typographic styles.

A third variable that has recently been introduced is the wide availability of *color* printers. Except for the most expensive models, these are almost always inkjet printers. The ability of these printers to reproduce photographic quality prints is stunning. Color can add a powerful impact to presentation materials and special printing jobs.

However, color is not yet readily accepted in formal correspondence, which is likely to be the heart of your personal promotion program. The color computers are also much slower than black and white printers and the colored inks add additional costs.

If you need multiple copies of a color photograph, reprints from your local drugstore are still superior to anything produced on an inkjet. In addition, the drugstore pictures are developed for you and don't require the use of your time.

Whatever you choose, be clear that people will judge you by the professionalism with which you present yourself. The power of a high-speed printer is also the power to embarrass yourself in front of large numbers of people. More important than what you use to print your message is how carefully you craft it, proof it, and present it.

Voice Mail

If you are part of a large corporation you are not likely to have much to say about what type of voice mail equipment is used. However, if you are in business for yourself, your decision about voice mail is an important one.

It may be as simple as an answering machine with multiple mailboxes. It may be the messaging service that is attached to your mobile telephone. Or, it may be a full service voice mail system offered by a private company or the various telephone companies. Only the largest companies are likely to own their own in-house voice mail system.

If you are charged with setting up a voice mail system for a small company, the most important thing you can do is to assure that the various menus are logically and comfortably structured for persons calling your firm. Continually examine your voice mail messages to assure that they are user-friendly and project the type of image you wish to have for yourself and for your company.

Voice mail as a personal promotion tool is mainly valuable for its speed and ease of use. However, used improperly, it may negate all the other personal promotion tools and efforts that you employ

Exhibit 7B shows how to make your personal voice messages more effective in presenting yourself to strangers. Many of the tips will also improve your messages to friends and co-workers.

Exhibit 7B: Best Practices For Voice Mail

☑ Speak slowly and don't rush your message. The thought that they are being recorded seems to make some people speak in bursts. Remember the listener is using only one of the senses to receive your message. And, s\he is probably trying to write and listen at the same time.

☑ Speak confidently. The sound of your voice is all the listener has to judge you. You want to create as good an impression from your message as you would from a personal meeting.

☑ Spell your name. It may be familiar to you but not necessarily to the listener. Even common names may have more than one spelling.

☑ Always repeat your name and your telephone number – once at the beginning and once at the end of the message.

☑ If you say you will call again, be certain to do so. The listener may be interested in your message but be waiting for your return call.

☑ If the listener does not know you, give a reason for your call. If you think the person you are calling will be reluctant to take\return you call, try to think of a provocative explanation that will interest the listener.

Facsimile Equipment

The ubiquitous FAX machine was really the first true electronic marketing tool. Long before E-mail was commonly available, people had old, smelly, slow FAX machines that could transmit a facsimile of a page around the world.

The FAX has some powerful advantages as a personal promotion tool. Your FAX machine has the ability to speak with virtually every other FAX machine in the world. You don't have to be concerned if they have E-mail, websites, comparable software, enough storage capacity or the right type of computing equipment.

It can present graphics, albeit rather crude ones. It can present a physical document carrying your message, rather than just the bits and bauds of an E-mail message. And it can do all this within seconds.

The most powerful aspect of FAX technology involves its ability (with the proper software) to send multiple FAXs directly from your computer to distant FAX machines.

Even better, all these capabilities are available through your personal computer, with an inexpensive Fax\Modem card.

Personal Promotion Software

Once you have the hardware in place, your next task is to select the software that you will use to manage your personal promotion program. You may choose from a wide range of excellent, low cost software. Contact managers, time management programs, data base managers, and personal information managers – all are powerful personal promotion tools. In addition, they are superior tools for the *individual* that is working alone to manage a personal promotion effort.

It can be argued that today's software programs are even better for use by a single individual than by a large corporation. Once you have to consider enterprise-wide solutions, software becomes much more complicated. The integration and communication requirements of the enterprise place a significant burden on the operation of the programs.

As the manager of your personal promotion campaign *you* control the power of personal productivity software. It serves only you.

Contact Managers

In one sense, the selection of software for your personal promotion program is very simple. There is a category of software that is specifically designed to do exactly what you wish to do: the *contact manager*. There are a number of programs that provide professional contact management, but no doubt the best known are ACT! and Goldmine. Almost any contact manager will do a creditable job for you. Whichever one you choose (and the most common ones are listed in Exhibit 7C,) you will find that they essentially all strive to provide the same capabilities:

- ☑ They record personal information about the individuals you wish to contact

- ☑ They record the various types of contacts you make with the individual

- ☑ They provide some way to prepare contact correspondence documents

- ☑ They help you keep track of tasks and projects

- ☑ They keep a calendar of past and future contact efforts

Exhibit 7C: Contact Manager Programs

- ☑ **ACT!** Symantec Corp. 800-441-7234, 541-334-6054; www.symantec.com
- ☑ **Day-Timer Organizer 2000**, Day-Timers Inc. 800-805-2615, www.daytimers.com
- ☑ **Goldmine**, Goldmine Software, Inc. 800-739-3884, www.goldminesw.com
- ☑ **Maximizer**, Multiactive Software, Inc., 888-577-7809, 604-601-8000, www.mizimizer.com

Built-in Or Added-On Contact Manager

Once again your corporation (in the selection of an enterprise-wide contact management system) may already have made this decision. Even if a comprehensive contact system is not in place at your company, you are likely to have among your desktop computer tools, either Lotus Organizer® or Microsoft Outlook®.

These are not full blown contact managers. However, their ready availability, their tight integration with the other desktop computing tools, and the continual improvement that has been made in their capabilities, makes them strong candidates for your personal promotion contact manager.

Defining Your Contact Record

Whether you are using the built-in desktop programs or an add-on contact manager, defining your contact record is already partially done for you. However, any program will allow you to customize the contact record to a greater or lesser degree to meet whatever specific requirements you may have.

For the type of activities in which you will be involved in your personal promoting program, almost any contact record will be suitable. Remember that you do not have the burden of integrating contact information with corporate sales and transaction information. That is the province of the enterprise-wide system.

You are simply developing lists and facts that will facilitate your personal contacts and correspondence with the people that are important to you and your career.

Nevertheless, it is useful to consider the type things that are contained in a contact record because they also suggest ways that you may use your contact management system. Exhibit 7D illustrates the basic elements in a typical contact record.

Exhibit 7D: A Typical Contact Record

☑ Title	☑ E-mail3 Address
☑ First Name	☑ Company Website
☑ Last Name	☑ Personal Website
☑ Suffix	☑ Admin Assistant
☑ Salutation	☑ Admin Assistant's
☑ Position	Telephone
☑ Company	☑ Supervisor's Name
☑ Department	☑ Supervisor's Position
☑ Business Address	☑ Pager Number
☑ Business City\State\Zip	☑ Home Address
☑ Business Telephone	☑ Home City\State\Zip
☑ Business FAX	☑ Home Telephone
☑ Mobile Telephone	☑ Home FAX
☑ E-mail Address	☑ Hobbies
☑ E-mail2 Address	☑ Spouse's Name
	☑ Children's Names

One of the best ways that you can customize your contacts is to group them in categories so that you may conveniently send messages to them that are most likely to be of interest. Exhibit 7E suggests one way that you might wish to categorize your contact records.

Exhibit 7E: Categories of Contacts

☑ Customers
☑ Ex-Customers
☑ Prospects
☑ Personal
☑ Trade Press
☑ General Press
☑ Associations
☑ Association Executives

☑ Corporate (your company)
☑ Competitors
☑ Printers
☑ Specialties
☑ Ad Agencies
☑ PR Agencies
☑ Web site designers
☑ Customer Service
☑ Audio Visual

Building Your Contact File

Who goes into your contact file? *Everyone.* At least everyone with whom you come in contact.

It is foolish to think that only people "important " to you are included in your personal promotion contact records.

☑ How can you tell who is going to be important to you in the future?

☑ How do you know where they may go in their career?

☑ How can you be sure what you may wish to do in the future?

If you have any type of contact with a prospect, a customer, a vendor, a representative from the media, it is only a slight additional effort to manage that contact through your contact manager -- as opposed to simply dashing off an E-mail or FAX or letter.

Once you have them as a part of your contact system all subsequent contacts are much more easily managed. Many times, what may seem a one-time contact will grow into a relationship requiring more frequent contacts.

The most important entries you will make in your contact file are those that come to you in the course of your day-to-day activities.

These are the contacts with which you have some association. If they receive correspondence from you they are most likely to remember you from the personal contact. Clearly all of these contacts are prime entries into your contact management file.

However, there may be people with whom you have had no personal contact that you want in your records. These might include certain vendors, association executives, and the news media.

Always be on the lookout for directories from professional organizations, trade associations, conferences and conventions. All these can provide valuable sources of contact information. In addition, they are likely to be up-to-date since the individual has recently volunteered the information.

> **If you have access to a document scanner, you may find that you can use its optical scanning (OCR) software to automatically convert printed directory records into digital contact records.**

E-mail Addresses And FAX numbers

Always collect E-mail addresses and FAX numbers even if you have no current plans to use them. These two pieces of information are the keys to *low cost* contacts with individuals.

> **Sending an E-mail may be totally without direct cost to you. A FAX can be sent for just a few cents.**

The cost of a first class stamp and the accompanying expense for the paper products that must be used make personalized letters an important, but increasingly expensive contact method.

Details Of Contact Events

The details of contact events can be viewed as simple memory aids. When did you last call this person? When did you send an E-mail? Which document did you mail to them?

If you have an excellent memory you might recall all these events. However, as your personal promotion plan progresses and the number of people you contact increases, you are probably more likely to need some type of formal record of contact events.

Even more important, formally recording your contact events will help you better plan how to create these events.

The standalone contact management programs excel at tracking these kinds of events. They will automatically prod you to schedule the next contact based on the date of the current contact.

However, even a *desktop communication tool* such as Microsoft's Outlook® provides a similar capability. Through a device called a "journal," it not only will track contact events, but various other documents and records on your computer that might be associated with this individual contact.

The important benefit is the record keeping. Without some facility to keep these records there is no way to bring organization and planning to your personal promotion efforts.

Calendar Of Contact Events

An important aspect of your decision to undertake a personal promotion program is an understanding that a successful program will require that you *create* contact events that might not occur by chance. Your objective is to raise your visibility with the contact audience.

Consequently, just as advertisers create <u>sale events</u>, you will create <u>contact events</u> as an excuse to contact your target audience.

For those contacts that occur naturally, your task is simply to handle them as professionally as possible. Even the way you compose and organize a simple E-mail is an opportunity to impress the recipient with your skills and professionalism.

However, an important part of your personal promotion plan is to design and structure opportunities to execute your personal promotion program. Exhibits 7F, 7G & 7H suggest the type of contact events you might create for different contact categories.

E-mail Systems

E-mail is one of the most important tools in any personal promotion plan and everyday it gets better. E-mail has some powerful advantages:

☑ It is available essentially without cost to you.

☑ It is virtually immediate.

☑ It is becoming almost universal so you can expect whomever you wish to contact to have an E-mail address.

☑ It requires the least time and personal effort to employ of all your personal promotion tools.

Exhibit 7F: Contact Events For A Senior Executive

☑ Report on a convention trip

☑ Report on a training program attended

☑ Report of a customer's reaction to a new service or piece of equipment

☑ Customers comments about a competitor's equipment

☑ Report on content of speech given by competitor's executive

☑ Contact with a competitor's executive or employee

☑ Opportunity to save expenses by changing a company procedure

☑ Sharing copy of presentation you have prepared

☑ Copy of interesting news article about the industry

☑ Forwarding copy of a directory of industry contacts

☑ Forwarding a digital photograph of a new piece of competitor equipment

☑ Writing a letter of congratulations on a promotion

☑ Providing information about a hobby known to be of interest to the executive

☑ Writing a "thank you" letter for your promotion

Exhibit 7G: Contact Events For A Co-worker

☑ A thank you note for assistance

☑ A "best wishes" letter on their birthday, or significant personal event, or promotion

☑ A congratulatory letter on the anniversary of their arrival at the company

☑ Sending copy of a useful spreadsheet or word processing template

☑ Sending FAQ on competitor's equipment\service

☑ Sending digital images of new equipment

☑ Sending articles that you have found useful

☑ Copies of professional books, either gift or loan

> ### Exhibit 7H: Contact Events For The Press
>
> ☑ Any event that might constitute "news" -- new offices, promotions, new employees, new products.
>
> ☑ Copies of insightful industry articles
>
> ☑ Suggestions for article subjects for a reporter.
>
> ☑ Copies of industry directories
>
> ☑ Responses to articles written by reporter
>
> ☑ Non-confidential copies of FAQs and "white papers" on your company's products
>
> ☑ Descriptions of reorganizations that have taken place within your company
>
> ☑ Assistance in finding information resources

There are some disadvantages to E-mail. First, it's ugly. In order to have assurance of broad acceptability of your message among *all* E-mail systems, you will likely have to use ordinary text messages only – no pictures, no attachments, no special formatting.

It is true that more and more E-mail systems are beginning to accommodate a broad variety of attachments. The attachments have the potential to be as elaborate as any other document you can prepare on your desktop: documents, spreadsheets, presentations, etc. However, these are enhancements you can only include when you know your recipient can accept them.

> **Noting a contact's capabilities as to reading E-mail attachments is an important enhancement to your contact record structure.**

However, no disadvantages for E-mail are significant when compared with its advantages to you: low or no cost to use, speed of delivery, serious (and perhaps immediate) attention from the recipient, ease of preparation, and its role as a superb tool to "broadcast" messages to a large group of people.

Avoid Spam

In E-mail circles, the worst accusation you can make is to identify a message of being "spam." The definition of "spam" varies by recipient. It is generally conceded to be any promotional message from someone unknown to you, which was not requested by you, and in which you have no interest. Most of the better E-mail systems have elaborate software designed to filter out spam E-mailing operations.

Regardless of our distaste for spam it is clear that E-mail is still becoming an increasingly important marketing communication tool. Most people do not object to receiving electronic promotional messages, so long as there has been some previously established contact with the sender, and some minimal level of interest in the content of the message.

Consequently, spam is beginning to be redefined more by timing, than content.

Certainly anyone to whom you send E-mail on your contact list — as a part of your personal promotion plan, should recognize your name. And once you have established this relationship, including them in your communication will seem a natural act – in fact, they may even appreciate it.

Always be certain that you have something of substance in any E-mail you send: news of the industry, news about a mutual acquaintance, a legitimate question, a personal comment that they will appreciate, etc.

In addition, consider the time and eyesight of your E-mail recipient. Use your spell checker, organize the logic and flow of your E-mail message, and don't send whole screens of dense, unbroken paragraphs.

The Power Of The BCC:

The E-mail that is sent to a large group of people listed in the E-mail's "To:" box is a staple of corporate communications. However, what if you don't want all your recipients to know who else received your message? An obvious promotional plan example of this would be if you were sending the same E-mail to your complete contact list.

There are stand-alone programs that do what is called "broadcast E-mailing" that will readily provide this option to you. However, for your homegrown "broadcast E-mail" system the ubiquitous "Blind Carbon Copy:" will serve very well. (Or should this be Blind Digital Copy?)

> **To use this tool, address your E-mail message to *yourself* and then list all the people you actually want to receive the E-mail as a "BCC:" recipient. Each will receive your message; none will know the names of the others on your list to whom it was sent.**

Personal E-mail Lists

To help you with your "broadcast" E-mails, personal E-mail *lists* are the solution. Just as you use "categories" of contacts to manage direct mail you may also use this same tool to manage your E-mail messages. Personal E-mail lists are a quick and efficient way for you to get your message broadcast.

Personal E-mail lists might include your department, your company (very powerful, and potentially dangerous), your special interest group, your personal Roundtable (see Chapter 9), your family, trade media, general media, and more.

Encryption Programs

Many E-mail systems have some facility for encrypting messages that are sent over the Internet. The subject of security in E-mail messages is a widespread concern in the industry. But until system-wide solutions are available, if you have a message that contains confidential information the only reasonably certain way to make it secure is to use an encryption program.

While few people are experts with encryption programs there is nothing very mysterious about them. The principles have been well known for many years. Through various systems they simply jumble your message on the sending end and reassemble it on the receiving end.

The factor that makes encryption programs so powerful today – even to ordinary users, is the speed at which desktop computers can manipulate the encryption algorithms. Consequently, this has made feasible the use of very complex algorithms. The ready availability of sophisticated encryption systems built on these algorithms are of serious concern to law enforcement and national security agencies. However, it is not your fault that these powerful systems are readily availability. If you need them, use them.

Encryption systems are usually described in terms of the size of the "key" that is used for encryption and decryption. The key is a sequence of characters that is used to control the encrypted replacement of the characters in your message. Common levels of keys are 40 bits, 56 bits, and 128 bits. Some commonly used encryption programs are listed in Exhibit 7I.

The most widely accepted algorithm for encryption on PCs is the RSA Data Security encryption scheme. This system is based on the difficulty of factoring very large *prime numbers.* The practical use of the system uses both a *public key* and a *private key.* An individual's public key is made known to all for *encryption* purposes. The private key is known only to its owner and is used for *decryption* purposes.

It is unlikely that any private person or enterprise has the computing or intellectual capability to "break" a 128-bit key. The capabilities of a country's national security agency is another matter, but they are not likely to be interested in your personal financial information, credit card numbers, old love letters, or personal promotion strategies.

Exhibit 71: Directory of Encryption Programs

- ☑ **Norton Your Eyes Only;** (Symantec Corp., 800-441-7234, www.symantec.com)
- ☑ **NovaStor-Authentex DataSafe;** (Novastor-Authentex Software Corp., 888-667-8228, www.authentex.com)
- ☑ **RSA SecurPC;** (Security Dynamics Technologies, 800-732-8743, www.securitydynamics.com)
- ☑ **SafeGuard Easy;** (Utimaco Safeware Systems Inc., 860-688-1199, www.utimaco.com)
- ☑ **SecureDoc;** (WinMagic, 888-879-5879, www.winmagic.com)

Project Management

Some of us feel that we are already overwhelmed just trying to manage one project – ourselves. Unfortunately, your boss is likely to believe that you should set your standards a little higher.

Most of the projects you are assigned to handle will be adequately managed with a combination of your personal calendar and your To Do list. But what if you have to manage something a little more complicated: less than the construction of a new building, but more than planning the boss's birthday party.

If your projects are really complicated, the decision is easy. Buy a professional project management program – Microsoft Project, CA-Superproject, etc. These are excellent and powerful programs that will track everything from rivets to rafters. However, they are not easy programs to learn and they are rather expensive. In addition, they use terminology and measures that primarily provide comfort to the skilled user.

You are likely to find that your bosses and subordinates will require that you frequently update them on your projects – and with terms and descriptions that are understandable to all.

Exhibit 7J lists most of the best-known project *management* programs. If you want just a sample of *project management lite*, the *project schedulers* such as Franklin Covey Company's On Target program will provide this for about $100.

If you don't need a professional project management program and your Personal Information Manager is not quite enough, you can still fall back on every businessperson's universal tool – the ordinary spreadsheet. You can always create a fairly useable project planning tools by keeping a spreadsheet with just five fields: Project Name, Date Started, Due Date, Task, Responsible, Notes. It's not pretty, but it's quick, easy, and available.

Exhibit 7J: Project Management and Scheduling Programs

- ☑ **CA-Superproject**. Computer Associates International; 800-225-5224, 516-342-5224; www.superproject.com
- ☑ **FastTrack Scheduler** (Project Scheduler), AEC Software Inc.; 800-346-9413; www.aecsoft.com.
- ☑ **Microsoft Project**, Microsoft Corporation, 800-426-9400, 425-882-8080; www.microsoft.com
- ☑ **Milestones, Etc.** (Project Scheduler), Kidasa Software; 800-765-0167; www.kidasa.com.
- ☑ **On Target** (Project Scheduler), Franklin Covey Corp. 800-877-1814; www.frannklinquest.com
- ☑ **Scitor Project Scheduler**. Scitor Corporation. 800-533-9876. www.scitor.com
- ☑ **Surtrak Project Manager**, Primavera Systems. 800-973-1335, 610-667-8600. www.primavera.com.
- ☑ **Time Line**, Time Line Solutions Corp. 415-898-1919. www.tlsolutions.com.
- ☑ **TodoManager** (Project Scheduler), Micro Logic Corp. 800-342-5930; www.miclog.com.
- ☑ **TurboProject Professional**, IMSI. 800-833-8082, 415-257-3000, www.turboproject.com.

Personal Promotion Paperware

We have reviewed personal promotion *hardware*, personal promotion *software,* but a third useful tool is personal promotion *paperware*. Regardless of the power of E-mail systems and FAX broadcasting, the reality is that people like to receive USPS mail. There is a pleasurable anticipation about opening a new letter -- even when you suspect it is simply another solicitation.

Personal stationary or *paperware* is a way for you to make a statement about the type of person you are. Do you prepare it with care? Do you craft your messages well? Do you send the correspondence on a timely basis? Do you present the message in an attractive and organized manner? Do you use paper products that are elegant and suggest the importance you place on the recipient?

Once again, the desktop computer and desktop printer are powerful tools in this effort. Personalization that was only available through expensive printing is now available to anyone. Printing your name and title on ordinary preprinted corporate stationary is as simple as typing the words.

Even better, use a form other than the standard 8 ½ x 11 corporate letterhead paper to get the recipient's attention. There are blank envelopes sold that fit exactly one-half of an 8 ½ x 11' sheet. This notepaper size is perfect for sending personal messages to your contacts.

There are also large "post cards" in this same 5 ½ x 8 ½' size that make attractive note cards. If you insist on traditional forms, you may buy folded note cards that will pass through your printer.

While your etiquette teacher and your mother may be appalled that you would use a laser printer to print any type of personal correspondence, you may not have the time to personally handwrite messages in your personal promotion program.

In addition, many of us have handwriting that is so atrocious that the message might not be readable even if you elected to hand write it. Use your laser printer. Just don't send it to your mother.

If money is no object and you want to make the best possible impression, have custom printed, personalized notepaper and envelopes. The old "executive" paper size of 7 ¼ x 10 ½ is still the most impressive and sophisticated letter that most people receive.

Business Cards - You Can Have More Than One

Almost everyone has a business card. Generally it identifies your position and association with a particular company. While this is the basic calling card there is no rule that says you have to be restricted to a single version.

Once again the desktop computer and printer come to our rescue. Blank card stock in ivory, gray, and white is readily available. Why not print up a *personal* calling card?

There is something ingratiating by giving someone a card with your home address, home telephone number, home FAX and E-mail address, rather than simply writing this information on the back of your business card.

Perhaps you have special interests – book collecting, baseball cards, an association in which you are an officer. Whatever your special interest, personal cards are likely to have greater impact on the recipient than one with the typical business information. Personalized cards are one more way to expand your circle of personal promotion.

Using The Web For Personal Promotion

The impact of the Internet and the worldwide web in recent years has been almost beyond belief. While all the "big money" interest is in its use in E-commerce, it may be that it is more powerful in its role as a communications medium.

We have already discussed the role of the Internet in external E-mail operations. However, the publishing of information for narrow audiences on websites may be an equally important role for the Internet.

Today there is virtually no interest so narrow that it does not have one or more websites devoted to it. All hobbies -- no matter how obscure, most organizations, all scientific interests and many families, have established websites.

> **The obvious question is would a person developing a personal promotion plan for business purposes, establish a <u>personal website?</u>**

A *personal* website – not a *corporate* website. If you are an entrepreneur or a professional there is a simple answer to this question of whether you should have a website -- absolutely. Even the smallest company can establish a simple website for very little cost.

However, it you are an individual working within a corporation the answer is probably "no." Someday personal websites will be accepted as a legitimate personal promotion tool, but today their use would likely be considered too obvious and crass.

This is not to say that there are no options for personal promotion on websites. Most corporate websites have "common drives" which all users may access to obtain useful instructions, calendars, and descriptive information.

The person responsible for preparing this information will likely welcome any assistance you offered to provide information to add value to the corporate files. Your listing as the contact person on this information makes the file a form of "signature token" (see Chapter 8). Even better, this "token" will be available to everyone in the company and the company will distribute it at its own expense.

In addition, there are likely to be trade or industry websites that have forums for comments from the public. Take a role in these discussions. If your contributions are rational, useful to other members of the forum, and pertinent to industry interest, you may become recognized as an opinion leader, solely from this activity.

Special Interest Websites

If your hobbies and special interests and industry associations play a role in your personal promotion plans, by all means take the initiative to prepare a website for these groups, if one is not available. As the "Sysop," you are, in effect, the editor of what appears on these websites.

You will see who is accessing the site. You will see what information is most popular. You will have a role in the focus of discussion groups. You may be consulted by the media as an authority on your special interest.

A tool in any activity is simply a way to expand the effect of an individual's efforts. Personal promotion tools certainly meet this definition.

The personal computer has opened Pandora's Personal Promotion Box, and we all sometimes suffer from its misuse. However, the skilled user applies the same talent and good judgment to the use of personal promotion tools as any other promotional activity.

The creation of a targeted contact base. The use of the right contact tool. The crafting of contact messages that contain information likely to be of interest to the recipient. The selection of timing that maximizes the effectiveness of the messages. These are the hallmarks of an effective promotion plan.

Choose and invest in personal promotion tools as you would any other important career enhancement tool. The costs are relatively low. The rewards can be life-long.

Chapter 8

Developing
Signature Gifts

In the beginning there was the ballpoint pen.

The poor old ballpoint pen has become the stereotypical cheap (and probably ineffective) premium. Everyone has a drawer filled with pens personalized with some company's name.

While a personalized ballpoint pen would be seen as a trite and obvious promotional ploy for an individual's personal promotion program, the marketing logic behind its creation and distribution is as sound today as ever.

Your task is to develop a signature gift or token that you can offer your friends and contacts, that is not quite so common or obvious as a ballpoint pen. You want people to remember you, your presence, your contributions, your availability.

> **The most effective personal promotion plan is one that is invisible to all but you. Distributing a signature token comes very close to revealing the workings of a personal promotion plan.**

Consequently, you should use these gifts with caution. If you cannot come up with a unique and useful item, it is probably better to use nothing at all.

Try to find items that can be *changed* to some degree before you give them to the recipient. It's better if everyone does not receive exactly the same item.

Having stated all these cautions, personal gifts and tokens still can be powerful ways to remind people of you and your activities within an industry. In addition, there are many ideas that only require your time to develop that would be appreciated by many of your contacts. Here are some ideas to get you started:

☑ **Digital Postcards** –We've already discussed the use of digital images attached to E-mails that might be sent upon your visit to a trade show. No one would object to receiving such items and would likely appreciate your thoughtfulness at including them in publicizing interesting things you have discovered.

☑ **Directory of Industry Events** –We all receive directories throughout the year from trade associations. Our primary interest is in resolving conflicts that may appear between these a number of different trade events. Perhaps a calendar that consolidated dates and locations of various events, at different trade associations, would be appreciated by your contacts.

☑ **Set of Industry Rolodex® Cards** –While most of us may be moving to computerized information systems, many of your customers may still use rotary card systems. Once you have developed a directory of industry contacts it is easy enough to use a copier or printer to print additional sets of these cards and distribute them on a regular basis to your contact list. You might even add your own name to each card as the contact for updates.

☑ **Set of Industry Contact Business Card Facsimiles** –You might offer your contacts a choice between rotary cards and business card facsimiles. Perhaps your contact would prefer to receive a card that would fit a business card folder rather than a rotary card file. It's the same information printed a different way.

☑ **Industry Reference Files** –If you see that a broad range of people uses certain statistics about your industry, you could be the person who collects and distributes this reference information. Maybe it's a printed report. Maybe it's a spreadsheet file that will allow further manipulation by the recipient. Maybe it's an E-mail bulletin you prepare and distribute.

☑ **"Free" Postcards** – Some companies already distribute free postcards. Hotels and motels have always done this. The postcard carries an attractive image, but allows the user to add personal information.

An individual that distributed free postcards would have to remove all "commercial" elements from the card. However, if you were a talented photographer, and the picture on the postcard was an attractive image that you created, your associates very well might appreciate the cards as small gifts.

Perhaps the postcard picture is a picture of something connected to your hobby; a picture of a local landmark; an illustration of a new industry process; a cartoon about a business situation.

☑ **Custom Screen Savers** – Several years ago, the production of customized screen savers was a popular premium item. They are less popular these days, as most people have simply decided to accept one of the standardized screen savers offered by the computer manufacturer.

However, if you can create a customized screen saver that has an image that is of particular interest to the recipient – an industry event, a special golf outing, a picture of an item used in the recipient's hobbies, a picture of the recipient's children – all of these items would add special interest to a gift screen saver.

Production of screen savers is very easy

with the ready availability of scanners and digital cameras. Any Microsoft Windows manual will describe how to create them.

☑ **Laminated Luggage Tags** –These items are traditional premiums but they still have value to most recipients. A key element is the use of the recipient's own business card to produce the tags. It seems that most of us have an increasing number of luggage, golf bags, equipment cases, etc., that all benefit from a personalized tag.

An alternative -- and less impressive, use of the laminated card is to create a facsimile of the recipient's calling card on your printer. This card is then laminated rather than the actual business card.

☑ **File of Industry Graphics** - We all have an insatiable need for images to illustrate and add interest to our presentations. Anyone would appreciate receiving a selection of images that represent objects commonly used in a particular industry.

While graphics files are very large in general, the low screen resolution required for most PowerPoint® presentations allows a number of files to be included on an ordinary 3½ inch diskette. Printing the paper label of the diskette allows for the personalization you need to associate this gift with you.

☑ **Reference Books/Booklets** –Once again you have the "power of the press" available right on your desktop. If you can develop an annual booklet of industry information, it can be inexpensively published and personalized with your name and contact information.

☑ **Diskette of Industry Facts and Figures** - An alternative to a printed document is simply to capture and distribute industry information in commonly read spreadsheet and database formats. In this way, the recipients may put this information to whatever use they choose.

The label of the diskette is your calling card. If the reference information file size is very large, you may have to use a CD. However, even custom CDs can be duplicated for only a few dollars each.

☑ **Directory of Industry Oriented Website Addresses** –The Internet is a vast storehouse of information. The problem most people have is fighting their way through it to find those specific websites of interest to them. You can become the guide and director to these interesting websites for your contact list.

Perhaps your annual compilation will become *"Dave's Recommended Websites for the Widget Industry."* The creation of this information only takes a little time on your part. The duplication of the paper document or the diskette that contains the information is a very low cost premium and something that cannot be readily duplicated by others.

☑ **Custom PowerPoint Templates** - The PowerPoint® presentation has become pervasive throughout the business world. This means that the standard templates provided by Microsoft have become well known to all.

The *smart presenter* designs custom templates in order to gain some small advantage in capturing the viewer's attention. The smart *personal promotion user* designs custom PowerPoint templates as gifts for important contacts.

Creation of a custom template is a fairly simple effort. An obvious device to customize the template is to add the recipient's name and corporate logo. (Generally, if the recipient's company has a website, you can copy the logo from there.)

Even better, change the colors to fit the corporate colors used at the recipient's company. Perhaps the template could have a background image of the recipient's logo or corporate headquarters.

While this type of token is likely to be more difficult to develop it is also more likely to be remembered by the recipient.

☑ **Words Of Wisdom** – Maybe your signature token should be providing your contacts a few insightful quotes or words of inspiration. Many people attach their titles or telephone numbers to the standard signature blocks that are automatically added to the bottom of messages sent by E-mail programs.

A better choice might be to select a series of relevant quotations at the bottom of your E-mails, FAXs and Memos. Even if you are not smart enough to write these pithy sayings, you can demonstrate your good taste and judgment by the quotations you select. Just remember to change them frequently.

What's useful? - All of these examples are simply to stimulate your thinking. The best token is one that is unique to you, not readily duplicated by other people, and is currently unused within your industry. Your personal computer and your desktop printer are your key to creating memorable signature gifts.

Chapter 9

Building A
Personal Success Roundtable

In addition to the millions of websites that populate the Internet, everyone has had some contact with the *Forums* and *News Groups* that were among the earliest users of the Internet. These groups are established around some specific interest to provide both reference material and an opportunity for discussion by anyone with an interest in the subject.

As the Internet has grown, these forums and news groups have splintered into ever smaller pieces so there is virtually no activity -- no matter how obscure, that does not support some interested population around the world that wishes to know more about it.

When you find a forum of interest, you are likely to be loyal to it over a long period of time -- even though an objective analysis would conclude that most of the information you read on the forum is of little real value to you.

A common problem is that many people have embraced the Internet as simply a way to gain some visibility for their thoughts and words, regardless how simplistic and banal they may be.

Nevertheless, you maintain your loyalty to your group because occasionally you find some nugget or insight or pleasure that makes it worthwhile, to fight your way through the other drivel that is posted.

Creating High Value Content

Given that you've seen that there are individuals and subjects that can provide valuable information to you:

☑ Why not try to find a way to build a forum that has a high percentage of this high value content?

☑ Why not seek out members of a forum that are like-minded and serious about the topic of interest to you?

☑ Why not ensure that the membership is controlled so that everyone feels a responsibility to make substantive contributions to its success?

> **One way to do this is to create a roundtable – nothing more than a small Internet forum, with a group of committed and knowledgeable members, to discuss an area of interest.**

Such a forum or *roundtable* is not going to be a tool directly associated with your *personal promotion* efforts. It is designed to provide an information resource for you, so that you are *smarter* about your personal promotion plan.

The other sections of this book largely require that you develop your own sources of information for decision-making and strategies. Your personal success roundtable can give you the opportunity to pool your knowledge with other roundtable members, in one or more areas that you have identified as useful in your development.

A roundtable can be established on any subject. While your primary interests are likely to be those subjects that contribute to your personal success and support your personal promotion program, there is no reason you cannot be involved in more than one roundtable in areas of interest to you – personal or business.

The requirements for such a roundtable are simple:

☑ The membership must all be like-minded and have an equally serious interest in the subject.

☑ The membership is limited and controlled to assure that personal accountability is maintained.

☑ The discussion for the roundtable is focused on a single subject during a specific time period.

☑ Potential discussion subjects are proposed by anyone in the group and selected based on a majority vote of the roundtable.

☑ One member of the roundtable will prepare a list of questions or a discussion outline so that the discussion will remain focused.

☑ Every member of the roundtable is required to provide information or commentary about the selected subjects, on a regular basis, by completing the outline\questionnaire.

☑ All of these activities are conducted over the Internet to ensure timeliness and ease of distribution.

☑ The members' contributions are compiled by a Moderator and made available to all the Roundtable members.

Perhaps this seems like a lot of trouble just to talk to a group of like-minded professionals. Why not just gather members for lunch at a local meeting room. Isn't this how "roundtables" have always been handled?

The luncheon meeting may seem a simple solution but it lacks a number of advantages available from the electronic roundtable:

☑ It requires everyone to dedicate a specific time period to the meeting. With the electronic roundtable, E-mail is available at each member's convenience.

☑ People are social animals. It is only natural to broaden matters discussed in a group meeting. E-mail communication is more focused.

☑ Verbal communication is less precise than written communications.

☑ Verbal communication leaves no written record to form useful archives.

There are plenty of opportunities to enjoy social meetings. Save your roundtable for business.

Recruiting Members

Once you have determined the focus of your roundtable, your first task is to recruit like-minded members to be members of the roundtable. With a "personal success roundtable" these are likely to be persons of *similar age* and at *similar points in their career.*

While you might have interest in the comments of a person very senior to you, that person may have less interest in *your* thoughts. Consequently, this would likely make this senior person less interested in supporting the roundtable and continuing to contribute to its discussions. Similar interests and similar stages in a career are best for a personal success roundtable.

> **Obviously, you are going to need to find people who are not directly competitive to your own ambitions.**

A good number of people for an effective discussion is eight to ten. However, if you found as many as four like-minded people you certainly could create the roundtable and use its activities as a tool to recruit additional members.

A questionnaire is an effective tool for recruiting members. You may even find that you have more interested candidates than one roundtable can manage. In that case, you can use the questionnaire to assist with the organization of multiple roundtables.

The example we are going to use in describing the roundtable structure is one that might be set up by a group of freelance copywriters. Freelance copywriters often feel isolated since most of the time they do not operate within the fraternal structure of an advertising agency or a corporation. They oftentimes deal with their clients over great distances. Nevertheless, this is a group that has common interests that lend themselves to the roundtable structure.

Exhibit 9A is the Membership Questionnaire developed for the Copywriters Roundtable.

Exhibit 9A: Membership Questionnaire for the Copywriters' Roundtable

Please complete this Profile and send by private E-Mail to:Mark Moderator (MModerator @hotmail.com)

Personal Information
- ☑ Name:
- ☑ E-MAIL Address:
- ☑ Snailmail Address (Optional):
- ☑ City/State/Zip:
- ☑ Telephone (Optional):
- ☑ Other Personal Information (Optional):

Work Experience:
- ☑ Number Of Years Copywriting/Staff or Freelance:
- ☑ Are you a full-time freelancer?
- ☑ If you work as a staff copywriter, at what type of company are your employed?
- ☑ Estimate the amount of your business that is devoted to the following media: Print advertising: Broadcast advertising: Direct Mail: Collateral: Speech Writing: Non-fiction books/articles: Fiction books/articles: Other/Describe

Industry Experience

Estimate the percentage of your business that is devoted to the following industries:

☑ Banking:
☑ Consumer:
☑ Distribution:
☑ Manufacturing:
☑ Medical Services:
☑ Other Financial:
☑ Other/Describe:
☑ Professional Services:
☑ Transportation:

Table Rules

One of the things that make Internet forums and news groups of less interest to professionals is their chaotic nature and absence of any real rules.

Consequently, so that everyone understands how activities will be conducted and so there is no misunderstanding about each person's responsibilities, the roundtable should begin with establishing a small number of critical rules.

The table rules for the Copywriters Roundtable (CWRT) are listed as Exhibit 9B.

Exhibit 9B: The CWRT Table Rules

☑ Minimum *number of members* is four, target is ten, and maximum is 12.

☑ *New members* will be recruited, as members are lost.

☑ Failure to submit *Topic Reponses* for three consecutive times is an automatic drop from the roundtable's roster.

☑ The position of *Moderator* will rotate at least every twelve months.

☑ The Moderator will assign the development of the monthly Topic Outlines to individual members of the Roundtable.

☑ The membership will be *polled* by the Moderator for any required decisions.

☑ *Required decisions* will be made by a majority of members voting.

☑ Members on the CWRT shall be non-competitive in local markets.

Table Topics

While it is assumed that members of a roundtable have *common interests*, it cannot be assumed that they have *equal interest* in subjects, at the same time.

Consequently, it's necessary to decide in what sequence points will be discussed by the roundtable. The roundtable might begin by the moderator (generally the founder of the roundtable) selecting an initial topic and proposing a series of subsequent topics for the first roundtable discussions.

After the initial subject is selected, a poll of the members for future projects would be a regular part of the roundtable notes. Topics should be planned three months in advance and a majority vote would decide the fourth month's topic.

The Roundtable Moderator

The first moderator of the roundtable is likely to be the person who founded it. There's likely to be no one else who has the interest to get it organized and to establish the necessary procedures. Responsibilities of the "Table Moderator" are fairly simple.

The moderator provides a modest amount of organization by maintaining certain roster information as well as compiling the various comments received from the members about the subjects under discussion. A moderator might serve for a period of one year and then the new moderator elected (or drafted!) by a majority vote of the roundtable.

The Roundtable Bulletin

Each month, the moderator would prepare a roundtable bulletin. This is little more than a cover sheet for the compiled responses about the previous month's subject. It includes a current table roster, miscellaneous table notes, a schedule of upcoming topics, a list of possibilities for future topics and the compiled responses from the roundtable membership about the previous month's subject.

A sample of the electronic bulletin from the Copywriters Roundtable is attached as Exhibit 9C.

Roundtable Response Outline

As indicated previously, a roundtable is a *focused discussion*. It is designed to avoid the dreaded "thread drift" that is so common among Internet discussion activities.

The primary way that responses are kept focused on the selected subject is through the use of a "Response Outline." With this tool, every member's response is provided in the same order so that organization and compilation of responses is made easy. A sample CWRT response outline is included as Exhibit 9D.

Exhibit 9C: The CWRT Bulletin

For February, 2000

Table Moderator: Mark Moderator- E-mail: MModerator@hotmail.com

Table Roster
John Doe / Atlanta, GA / E-MAIL: Jdoe@hotmail.com
Jack Roe / New York, NY / E-MAIL: Jroe@hotmail.com
. . .
Zack Zoe / 1442 Sprint St. / Raleigh, NC 28219 / 919-555-1212 / E-MAIL: Zzoe@hotmail.com

Table Notes
A. Jack Roe recommends that CWRT members limit topic responses to three pages and that samples, files, etc., beyond this length be put in attachments.

B. Karen Coe has moved. Her new Snail Mail address is: 1234 Main St., Jackson, MS 39123 / 601-555-1212.

C. The compiled files from the January Topic have been made a part of the Roundtable's archives and are available to any member upon request.

Upcoming Topics:

March Topic Title: Direct Mail For New Business
March Topic Outliner: Mark Moderator
March Topic Deadline: March 5, 2000

April Topic: Computer Programs For Copywriters
April Topic Outliner: John Doe
April Topic Deadline: April 5, 2000

May Topic: Finding Health Insurance
May Topic Outliner: Deb Roe
May Topic Deadline: May 5, 2000

Poll For June Topic

Reorder the following proposed topics to your order of preference. Submit this reordered list with your response to the March topic.

- *Creating A Professional Image With Your Documents*
- *How To Collect The Funds And Still Keep The Client*
- *Letters Of Agreement With Sub-Contractors*
- *Ways To Introduce Increased Prices*

Submit proposed future topics to Mark Moderator at *MModerator@hotmail.com*

Exhibit 9D: Sample Roundtable Response Outline

The Copywriters Roundtable

Topic: Direct Mail For New Business

Response Due Date:	*March 5, 2000*
Topic developed by:	*Mark Moderator*
Submit by private E-mail to:	*Mark Moderator*

CWRT Member: *(Enter your name here)*
CWRT Member E-MAIL Address: *(Enter your E-mail address)*

Response Outline:

☑ How important is direct mail to the new business efforts of the free-lance copywriter?

☑ Describe your use of direct mail for new business in the last 12 months.

☑ Describe your most successful use of direct mail for new business.

☑ Describe the best use of direct mail by any copywriter for new business that you have seen.

☑ How do you integrate direct mail into your other new business efforts?

☑ Describe any samples that you would be willing to share with CWRT members through Snail Mail.

☑ Other Comments

Do You Have Questions?

While the primary focus of the roundtable is to directly gather information from the experience of the roundtable members, it can sometimes be useful to allow roundtable members to pose questions based on the responses they read.

> **Of course, questions and comments are the elements that lead to those interminable discussions on the Internet discussion groups that seem to go on and on, about less and less.**

Consequently, a useful rule is to allow a single series of questions about a member's comments. If two members wish to discuss a topic in greater detail this would then become a personal exchange between these two and not involve the roundtable activities.

A Roundtable *And* An Archive

While the primary focus of the roundtable is on the roundtable members' opinions and experiences, a compilation of roundtable responses also becomes a valuable resource. New members may join the roundtable and wish to review past discussions. Roundtable members may wish to revisit certain topics and review the past discussion as a springboard for greater discussion.

It's the responsibility of each moderator to maintain the files of the roundtable. The most immediate responsibility is to compile each month's responses into this month's discussion. But once these compilations are made, they become a part of the roundtable archives.

> **The fact that the roundtable uses an outline to focus discussion and comments keeps discussion on target, and makes it easier for the moderator to compile the monthly responses.**

The Moderator simply sorts the responses by the question included in the roundtable outline. Any subsequent questions or comments about the members' responses are added into the discussion report before it is placed in the archives.

Topic Sequence

The monthly cycle of the roundtable's activities are as follows:

- ☑ The moderator and/or members propose topics for discussion
- ☑ Topics are selected for three months in advance
- ☑ Topics for the fourth month are voted upon by the roundtable members
- ☑ One roundtable member is appointed by the moderator to prepare a topic outline for

each subject, in order to *focus responses* on the most useful information to the Roundtable members

☑ Roundtable members are required to respond to each month's topic by a specific due date and in the context of the outline that has been prepared

☑ The members' responses are reported by the moderator to each member of the roundtable by E-mail

☑ One level of questions are allowed between members about each other's responses

☑ Questions and responses are incorporated in the final report by the moderator and placed in the archives

☑ The next roundtable bulletin is sent to the roundtable membership and the cycle begins again

So You Won't Be Lonely On Your Way To The Top

Roundtable groups can be important sources of information as well as provide opportunities to expose your thoughts to objective and qualified commentators. Even your spouse is not likely to share your intense interest in some obscure subject that is important to your personal promotion plan. A roundtable provides mutual benefit to all its members, and provides information and discussion that may not be available from any other activity in which you are involved.

Chapter 10

Preparing a
Personal Promotion Plan

To this point we have talked about the various tools that you might employ in your personal promotion effort - objectives, timing, strategies and resources. Like any organized activity, your personal promotion effort requires that you develop a plan – a written plan. Why written? Isn't it enough that you know what is your plan?

Putting things in writing adds improved organization to your efforts. The human mind is fallible. It cannot remember everything it considers.

Putting a plan in writing allows you to collect your thoughts, collect valuable information and collect ideas. It also will help you expose weaknesses and omissions from your plan.

> **This is not to say that your personal promotion plan is a static document. You must continually revise it as you succeed or fail, as you get additional information, and as events require adjustments.**

You are not the only one in your various circles that has ambitions and objectives. Their activities will affect yours. At least once a month (preferably weekly,) you should review your plan, measure what progress you have made and adjust it as necessary.

A Plan That Is Obvious Only To You

The development and execution of a personal promotion plan is not something you should discuss with co-workers anymore than you should discuss a company's marketing plan with competitors.

It is a personal plan. It's as intimate as a diary. It identifies ambitions and strategies that you should reveal only to your closest relationships.

> **Developing and executing a personal promotion plan is an activity that you do not wish to be obvious to the casual observer. You are attempting to affect other people's activities. You are trying to influence their judgment about corporate decisions.**

No one wishes to feel that they have been unduly influenced or manipulated in their decision-making.

That's why although everyone admits to seeing advertising, no one will admit to actually having been influenced by it. You want the targets of your promotion plan to be equally oblivious to your efforts.

Elements Of Your Plan

A personal promotion plan is not significantly different from any other marketing or business plan. It has the same elements. It is simply necessary to interpret them to fit their very personal purposes.

Every plan must have specific *objectives*. These should be stated in a manner consistent with the time frames in which you hope to meet them. You might have *career* objectives, *three-year* objectives, *one-year* objectives and *thirty-day* objectives.

In addition, you will have specific *tactics* you plan to employ to meet these objectives. These tactics will determine both the actions that are taken and the resources you plan to employ.

> **A personal promotion plan that is primarily focused on visibility and awareness will necessarily have contact information as a primary component.**

You should identify both primary and secondary contacts that are required for the success of your plan. Often, it will be necessary to identify mutual acquaintances or *secondary* contacts in order to make a *primary* contact aware of your activities. Identifying these *secondary* contacts is a necessary first step in order to obtain the awareness of your primary contact.

A *budget* should be considered for your personal promotion activities. While you won't be buying advertising or investing in new capital equipment (except for your computing equipment,) there will be necessary expenditures.

You may have *entertaining* that has to be done, *printed materials* that have to be created, *signature tokens* that have to be purchased and other expenses that may be necessary in order to execute your plan. Developing a budget for these items requires you to confirm to yourself the importance of these activities and your willingness to invest in them.

> **It is the significant events in your personal and corporate life that will largely govern opportunities in your career.**

Significant events in your life and your company's life should be carefully tracked. If you allow yourself to come to work each day and be surprised by the day's events, you will never be able to *take control of those events.* You must develop planning horizons that allow you to *anticipate events* and take those actions that are necessary for the execution of your plan.

Finally, all of these activities should be coordinated by a *personal promotion calendar.* You are about to undertake an activity that is in addition to your primary business and personal activities. It is easy to postpone or rationalize not executing your personal promotion plan. After all, you already have a full life with myriad requirements.

The personal promotion calendar will help you identify those actions and activities that you must keep on track in order for you to succeed with your personal promotion effort.

A personal promotional plan will have emphasis on the *personal.* Everyone's situation, skills, ambition and opportunities are different. However, Exhibit 10A outlines an approach you can use until you develop your customized version.

Scheduled Events For Contact Targets

In Chapter 8, we reviewed examples of typical contact events that might be useful to you. *Scheduling* these contacts is what is necessary in order to create a personal promotion plan. There are no more important events in your personal promotion calendar than events that you schedule with your contact list.

One key difference with *scheduled* contacts in a personal promotion plan is that they may not be *personal* contacts. You should include contacts of all types – E-mail, letters, telephone calls.

Your objective is to assure <u>visibility</u> so that you are considered to be a part of the day-to-day activities of your contact list.

Obviously, if you are aware of personal events in their lives such as birthdays, promotions and other significant events, these also should be tracked so they are not omitted from your contact activities.

If there are social events where significant numbers of your contacts will be present, these also should be scheduled so that you can provide appropriate recognition and attention in your contact efforts.

Scheduling Contact Events With Your Management

The most important contacts you have are likely to be your company's management. While you will have certain natural, day-to-day contact with your managers and co-workers, your objective should be to take control of these events so that they are handled completely and in a manner consistent with your objectives.

Some contact events are both obvious and particularly effective in demonstrating your capabilities to your management. What follows is a description of events that are of particular interest to you and your personal promotion plan. In Exhibit 10B, a possible schedule for the timing of various contact events is included.

Weekly Or Monthly Status Reports

This is your *newsletter* to your management describing those activities that are fundamental to your success or failure. They should be carefully prepared and appreciated for what they are – a direct pipeline to the attention of your managers.

Joint Calls On Customers And Prospects

Managers are often flattered when you ask them to accompany you on a joint call with a customer or prospect. Most managers think they need to "spend more time in the field." The more senior the manager, the more likely they are to feel this need and the less able to satisfy it. By taking the initiative and requesting their assistance, you not only have a valid reason to schedule a contact event, you flatter them by indicating that their presence will be a positive event for your customer or prospect.

In addition, joint calls provide an excellent opportunity for your management to observe you in front of your customers and prospects and to see you in a role other than that of their subordinate.

Performance Reviews

It would seem logical that your performance reviews would be a key part of your planning horizons. However, this is among the least important things you need to track. All of your other activities are keyed to improving what you hear in a performance review. If you take care of these activities then the performance review should take care of itself.

Perhaps more important is that you should track the date that *your boss* is reviewed. It is before and after this point that your boss is likely to undertake significant activities that might affect you – good or bad. New initiatives, more critical reviews of your performance, additional contact with your boss's superiors, etc -- these are the events that will most likely affect you and your activities.

Budgeting Periods And Review Points

The modern corporation today is designed around predictability – predictability for its management and its stockholders. The chief financial officer of every company is charged with creating an ever-increasing income and profit flow in acceptable amounts. The primary tool with which this is accomplished is the corporate budget.

The budget can be both a threat to your activities as well as a source of resources to support your proposals. You must remain aware of the overall financial performance of your company. You can be certain that this is a daily consideration of senior management and that the conclusions they draw about these results will directly affect you and your activities.

Board Meetings

You have your monthly review meetings. Senior management has its monthly board meetings. These are meetings where significant initiatives must be introduced and approved by the board. These are also the times when senior management is most likely to be subjected to critical review.

You don't want to make the mistake of making proposals to management that requires significant risk when they are distracted by preparation for board meetings. Conversely, if financial results are positive, the board is happy, and management is secure, then they are more likely to be open to new proposals and commitments.

New Product Cycles

Most companies have some type of new products or planning activity. Old products die; new products must be developed to replace them.

Once again this is a time of significant risk for a company. Commitments have to be made. Options are foreclosed. Resources are committed. These activities are not only excellent opportunities to acquire visibility within your company; they are also significant events that should be tracked on your personal promotion calendar.

Advertising Schedules

An advertisement is to a corporation what a speech is to a corporate executive. It outlines what the company wishes others to believe. It is important in your planning calendar because it identifies what your management wants the community-at-large to know about the corporation and its activities.

Always be alert to any changes that are reflected in advertising that are contrary to your assumptions about management's objectives and positioning. What they may not personally tell you may be broadcast in the media and you should be sensitive to the information provided.

Competitive advertising is equally important. Competitive messages also provide insights into the thinking of your competition and provide useful information that you can use in your day-to-day competitive activities.

While advertising schedules may not be commonly known, they are rarely a secret. If you are inquisitive and alert, it is likely you can determine the dates of the advertising campaigns planned by your company and incorporate these in your promotion calendar.

Association Meetings And Conventions

We've previously considered the value of your involvement in association activities. Association meetings are always scheduled far in advance and can be easily incorporated in your calendar. They may range from monthly meetings of the local Chamber of Commerce to annual conventions of large trade associations. If you wish to be involved in these meetings, you must start planning for them many months in advance.

It is the association staff's responsibility to manage large conventions. An important tool the staff uses is the appointment of program and committee leaders for various elements of the convention. Program committees develop programs. Topics are selected months in advance. Program chairman and program committees are appointed to select speakers and speaker topics.

These are the type of planning activities that you must track if you want to play a serious role in a convention or conference. By the time the announcement is made to the public about the conference's activities, it's too late. All significant arrangements are already in place.

Whenever you attend a convention or conference, carefully study how it is organized, which executive staff members are involved and should be cultivated, how far in advance was the meeting planned. Estimate the times these activities will be undertaken for the following year and incorporate these dates into your promotion calendar.

Personal Time Scheduling

While this is primarily a book about personal promotion and personal success in your career, what is the point if there is not also time for success in your personal life? The events with your family and those other activities of personal interest to you deserve just as much attention and careful and considered scheduling as any other activity.

Why not employ the tools you are putting in place to track your business activities to ensure you do not overlook those significant family events, vacations and gatherings that are important to you? This will also help ensure that you do not schedule conflicting business activities that might detract from your enjoyment of personal activities.

Your personal promotion plan represents your most important commitment to taking charge of the actions and events that will most influence your career. There is no more important document you can prepare for yourself.

- ☑ It collects the best of your thinking.
- ☑ It provides a reference tool for your decision-making.
- ☑ It is testimony to your intention to excel.

Exhibit 10A: Outline For a Personal Promotion Plan

Plan Objectives & Strategies

☑ What do you hope to accomplish

☑ What will change as a result of the successful execution of the plan

☑ What are the benefits to the company

Current Situation

☑ Current company – Growing, stable or declining; Strength and weaknesses of industry and market in which it operates

☑ Company management – Attitudes toward you, mastery of market needs, acceptance of ambitious employees and rapid advancement

☑ Skill Set – Talents and skills that you have accumulated

☑ Weaknesses – Additional talents and skills that you need to develop

☑ Current position – Analysis of current position as platform for advancement

☑ Other positions -- Analysis of other possible positions as platforms for advancement

Personal Value Description

☑ A short statement describing your role, value, and skills as a successful employee

Competition

☑ Strengths and weakness of persons most likely to be your competitors for advancement

☑ Position each competitor's strengths and weakness against your own talents (i.e. computer skills, presentation skills, reputation, industry knowledge, verbal skills, writing skills, etc.)

Corporate Need Matching

☑ Primary immediate corporate needs -- Describe those solutions that are most needed for the company's immediate success

☑ Primary forecasted corporate needs -- Describe those solutions that are most needed for the company's medium and long-term success

☑ Match your existing skills and available solutions with the company's needs

☑ Identify those additional talents you must acquire to be in a position to help the company meet its needs

Communication Strategies

☑ Overall themes of communication messages to be employed

☑ Description of communication messaging to be employed with each contact segments (i.e. boss, boss's bosses, co-workers, industry, community)

Communication Targets Interests

☑ Identification of messages that are most likely to invoke positive responses from the target contact groups

Timing Of Strategies
☑ Dates on which specific tactics, actions, and contact events will be launched

Resources Budget
☑ Equipment needed to support promotional plan
☑ Information resources need to support plan (newspapers, professional magazines, professional books)
☑ Memberships and dues
☑ Costs of postage, signature gifts, printing
☑ Timing of investments

Community Activity
☑ Identification of community organizations in which you will be active
☑ Specific contributions you can make to each community organization
☑ Timing of important community events

Trade Activity
☑ Identification of industry organizations in which you will be active
☑ Specific contributions you can make to each trade organization
☑ Timing of important trade events, conventions and conferences
☑ Editorial calendars for important trade media

Documents\White Papers

☑ Identification of documents and white papers that will attract favorable notice

☑ Location of information resources required for white paper preparation

☑ Schedule of document preparation

Direct Mail\E-mails\FAXs\Other Impersonal Contacts

☑ Overview of strategies, goals, vehicles to be used and timing of "impersonal" contact messages

☑ Schedule of impersonal contacts

☑ Segmentation of contact groups to receive specific messages

Contact Channels

☑ Identify specific contact channels that will be employed in your plan

☑ Rank contact channels by relative importance

☑ Identify events to contact each channel

☑ Match contact efforts and contact channels

Success Metrics

☑ Schedule for regular review of plan, its validity, and required changes

☑ Expected time frames for success events

☑ Measures of success/failure

Consolidated Calendar

☑ A paper or electronic calendar that incorporates all events with scheduled or expected date

Exhibit 10B : A Contact Event Planning Matrix

Event – Weekly, Monthly, Annually, Random	W	M	A	R
Advertising Campaigns				☑
Annual Budget			☑	
Annual Review – Boss & Yours			☑	
Annual Reviews – Subordinates			☑	☑
Birthdays – Co-workers				☑
Birthdays -- Family			☑	
Board Meeting		☑		
Budget Review		☑		
Contact Events -- Community		☑		
Contact Events – Co-workers	☑			
Contact Events – Key Customers	☑			
Contact Events – Sr. Execs.	☑			
Contact Events – Trade		☑		
Customers – Budgeting Period			☑	
Customers – Key contacts review date				☑
Family Events				☑
Key Committee Meetings		☑		
Monthly Project Review		☑		
New Product Introductions				☑
Personal Promo Plan Review	☑			
Roundtable Due Dates		☑		
Seminars - Educational				☑
Stockholders Meeting			☑	
Trade Association Meetings				☑
Vacation – Personal				☑

Chapter 11

Ten Standards For Measuring The Plan You Build

A book such as this one necessarily includes a lot of recommendations and prescriptions. *How* to do something. *When* to do something. *Why* to do something. Keeping track of all these tasks can sometimes make your objectives seem further away, rather than closer.

But most of the activities discussed are already a part of your everyday life. Your job is to just learn to do these things *better*, and with *more purpose*.

You want to do them at a time they will do you the most good. You want to focus your efforts on targets that yield the most benefit to your career.

Regardless of the complexity of your personal promotion campaign, sometimes the most difficult task is to just take the first step.

> **That's why you should not try to plan *victory*. Just plan the steps that take you in victory's direction.**

Get your hardware and software tools in place. Work to improve your communication skills – one at a time. Build your contact list. You cannot do everything at once. You can only begin the process.

While the tools described in this book purposely have been very specific, there are broader concepts that should guide you as you execute your personal promotion plan. Here are some that you should consider.

Promotions Are Built On People, Not Positions

Most human activity is organized in one way or another – companies, associations, clubs, families. Regardless of the tools and rules and practices that an activity employs, it's all about dealing with people.

You can have the best tools, the best plan, the best intellect, but if you don't have the ability to effectively interact with the people with whom you come in contact, you will be restricted to a narrow and limited area of success.

While you are focusing on your *career* success, don't lose sight of the fact that *personal* success is always more rewarding.

People Grow. Careers Evolve.

Young people are often pushed and prodded and questioned about what "career" they are planning to have. The idea that a young adult is likely to select a career at an early age and actually achieve success in that career is one of the grosser misrepresentations that adults inflict on youth.

> **Interests change. Industries change. The world changes. A few years ago, who had heard of E-commerce and .COM companies?**

If you focus your career efforts on a single job or position, who is to say that it will even exist by the time you are ready to assume it? Build your skills. Build your professional equity. Maintain flexibility in your actions so that you may respond to whatever opportunities are presented to you.

You Manage Your Career, Not The HR Department

Some may think it unfair to charge that corporate Human Resource departments have become more builders of bureaucracies than builders of employees. Even if this charge is true, it is not necessarily because HR managers have planned it this way.

Labor law has become a minefield of charges, and lawsuits, and regulations. A major portion of any HR department's resources is devoted to keeping its company out of court and in compliance.

> **Regardless of whether modern day HR departments have been built by design or default, they should not be considered an ally of the ambitious employee.**

The fact that you manage to "stand out" may be enough for the HR department to view you more as a problem than a valued resource.

This doesn't mean that you can afford to ignore the HR department. If your actions or plans are contrary to some rule or regulation that governs employee and employer relations, you will lose. The penalties on companies for violating labor laws and regulations are too severe for a company to risk violation.

Also, you should be aware of the opportunities that are controlled by HR and maximize your use of these opportunities – training, cross-training, special advancement programs.

Your focus should always be that *you* are the "human resource" you are the most interested in improving and promoting. If you build your "resources," your managers will notice – and so will the HR department.

The First Step To *Achieving Success* Is *Assuming Success*

"Dress For Success" was offered as a key to success a few years. But just putting on a new suit is not quite enough. The covering you need to wear is a combination of determination, skills and actions.

If you want to achieve a particular position, determine what is *required from you* for that position. Don't assume that the position will be adapted to fit your particular qualities.

To obtain the new position, what must you know? What are the characteristics that others possessed who attained this position? What problems will the person holding this position be asked to solve. Whom must you satisfy? How must you conduct yourself? With whom must you work? And yes, how should you dress?

Adjust your skills, your actions and your manner to match the needs of the desired position.

Success Is Never 100%

Two hunters are walking through the woods. A bear rushes them and one of the men starts to run. The second man says, "You fool, you can't outrun a bear!" The first man says, "I know. I just have to outrun you!"

The running hunter was applying marginal differentiation. His marginal difference was to be faster than his partner. In maintaining your marginal differentiation, you will not have to achieve 100% superiority, just enough superiority that you surpass your competition.

> **All business decisions are choices among available alternatives. Your superiors will not promote you because they think you are perfect. They will promote you because they think you are the best among the choices available to them.**

This fact should suggest to you that it sometimes is counterproductive to continue to improve your skills in an area in which you are already superior. If you are already the Excel® whiz, perhaps you should work on your presentation skills. If your boss thinks you are a jewel, perhaps you should build your reputation with the other executives in the company.

Minimize Your Enemies. Maximize Your Friends.

If you are going to have any impact in your position, you are inevitably going to have some degree of conflict with some number of people. People have different objectives. People have honest differences of opinion. Perhaps you are right and they are wrong.

For whatever reasons, it is always possible that a conflict can grow to create an enemy. If the conflict involves a point of principle or a position that is important to you, then just accept the enemy as a natural byproduct of business. Anyone with ambition has some enemies.

The enemies you want to avoid are those you unnecessarily create, carelessly, without thinking, perhaps just because you lose patience with someone.

Some people seem to invite rebuke. They appear too lazy, too wrong or just too stupid to ignore. The question you should always ask yourself is, is it your responsibility to improve their performance? If not, let someone else do it.

Enemies are baggage on your road to the top. Don't carry any more than you must.

Build A Team Not A Tunnel

Building personal skills is a necessary part of your personal promotion plan. Improvements in written communications, technical skills, presentation skills all are important. The danger is that you may come to think that *professional skills* are all that is necessary for *professional success.*

There are very few activities in which you can be a success solely through your individual efforts. To succeed, you are going to need partners, support and cooperation.

> **The idea of managing your contacts --
> central to this book, is not just so your
> contacts can witness your successes.
> Your contacts are important because they
> may choose to help you achieve your
> successes.**

An inflated sense of superiority or an overreaching self-confidence, can lead you to ignore the benefits from organizing a circle, a department, a roundtable, -- a team that is working for your success.

Consider Carefully. Act Decisively.

One of the cautions that appears throughout this book is a warning about the power of personal promotion tools to both leverage your successes and *expose your follies.*

Personal promotion strategies are serious matters. They should not be afterthoughts or casual decisions. They are as important as any decision you will make for your company or your family. They deserve your careful consideration.

However, once you have made a decision, selected a strategy, and committed yourself, you must *act decisively.*

Never let fear that you have not yet discovered the <u>perfect strategy</u> keep you from taking decisive action with an <u>acceptable strategy</u>.

In the real estate business, it is said that there are three requirements for success – location, location, and location. In business management the corollary requirements for success are execution, execution, and execution.

An acceptable strategy that is *well executed* will generally succeed over a superior strategy that is *timidly executed.* This fact should not be hard to accept. What defines the best cola drink, or filled cookie or salted snack? Objective taste testing?

The marketing research industry is littered with products that *test best,* but *sell less.* Lesser products can succeed with *superior execution.*

Carefully select the best strategy you can, with the information that is available to you. *Confidently execute* the selected strategy.

Invest In Yourself Before The Market

Today, everyone seems to be a player in the stock market. When a market rises over a period of years, it can appear invincible. Rational people understand that this is not true.

Certainly, stocks are an important investment opportunity and estate-planning tool. But the most

important assets you can acquire are your
professional skills. Investments to improve and
enhance your skills will pay dividends whether the
stock market rises or falls, and regardless of how your
career may evolve.

> **Why would anyone believe that
> allowing strangers to invest your money
> in their businesses is somehow more
> secure than investing your money in your
> business – which is your career?**

You will certainly encounter obstacles in
achieving your career objectives. However, never let
these obstacles be ones created by the absence of
personal skills and training that you should have
provided by investing in yourself.

Your Job Is Not Your Title

Corporations have always exploited their
employee's desire for titles. The hierarchy of
corporate titles is carefully managed to maintain the
illusion that they represent the power structure
within the company.

But the real power structure in any corporation
(or any other kind of organization) is represented by
the value the corporation and its managers place on
the contributions of the individual employees.

Every corporation has "Senior Vice Presidents"
that have been simply parked with an impressive title

until retirement or termination. These *trophy titles* don't really represent power and influence within the corporation.

There is nothing wrong with aspiring and attaining a senior title, so long as you never forget how transitory a title can be. Remember that *you don't own the title.* It is the property of the corporation.

Your property is your reputation, your skills, your ability, and your professional equity. Always focus on maintaining your real value to the company and to its executives.

The final standard you should apply to your plan is this: is it working? Are your proposals accepted? Is your opinion solicited? Is your contact base expanding? Are you applying the necessary energy to your personal promotion plan? If any of the answers to these questions is "No," modify your plan, search for different tactics, redouble your efforts.

Whatever your plan, whatever your tactics, the core strategies don't change:

- ☑ **Keep your skills current.**
- ☑ **Keep your contacts active.**
- ☑ **Keep your contributions visible.**

Dave Marley may be contacted
by E-Mail at:
DMarley@compuserve.com

Additional copies of this book may be
ordered from
Silverpoint Press

Toll free <u>FAX or phone</u>:   1-888-467-5989

or by E-mail: 72335.724@compuserve.com

Notes

Notes

Notes